TASK FORCE A

AN ODYSSEY

For Ken and Doreen
with my best wishes
and gratitude for all
your help.

[illegible]

"It is better to light a candle than to curse the darkness"

As the first humanitarian aid arrives in Kavaja, just what is going through this little girl's mind as she stands on the wrong side of the barbed wire fence?

TASK FORCE
ALBANIA
An Odyssey

by

John van Weenen

First Published – August 1998

Acknowledgements:

The author wishes to thank – Bill Hamilton for his kind permission in allowing extracts from *Albania Who Cares?* to be reproduced. The many thousands of British people who responded so marvellously to the appeal for humanitarian aid. The dedicated group of voluntary workers who assisted him over a period of seven years: Alan Blake, Alan Bristow, Azad Kumar, Roy Richards, Gordon Collis, Michael Batten, Bob Poynton, Michael Randall, Bernard Coppen, Kenny Palmer, Mark and Elaine Seabrook, Sue Cowley, Irene Leslie, Darren Gill, Tim Eyrl, Annabel Studholme, John Dawson, Louise Cooper, Joanna Kettle, Steve Thompson, Joanna Snel, Roy Hazlewood, Jacqueline Maylem, Gursharan Sahota, Tony Benford, Richard Patterson, Greg Mort, David Fox, Arthur Tooms, Kym Watson, Carolyne Watson, Vic Kaye, Susan Thorn, Jane Sydenham, Pedro and Carol Barker, Stuart Bennett, Stephen Clay, Kevin Burton, Carolyn O'Donnell, Carol Rowley, Duane Courtney, Lorna Jepps, Dave and Mary Gregory, Trevor and Pina Cumberpatch and Jeffrey van Weenen.

All our Albanian friends, without whom we could not have carried out our work: Socol and Lindita Agolli, Sulejman and Tatjana Zhugli, Luiza and Thoma Dhamo, Agron Afezolli, Dr. Linda Ciu, Pjeter Arbnori, Ali Spahia, Prof. Dr. Sali Berisha and family, Bashkim Baholli, The Brahimi Family, Ledio Celiku, Maksim Cikuli, Vjollca Dedei, Dervish Duma, Tomor Dosti, Agron Hoxha, Fatmir Lacej, Ferit Hafizi, Luketa Hasa and Family, Krist Andon, Jehona Metaliaj, Dode Kacaj, Philip Logoreci, Doreen Logoreci, Mirush Mati, Pëllumb Malaj, Vangjel Dheri, Tritan Shehu, Shpresa Vreto, George Hysaj, Roland Xhaxho, Zana Harxhi, His Excellency Agim Fagu, Afrim Haci, Naske Afezolli, Pavli Qesku, Artan Spahiu and all at the Albanian NGO Forum in Tirana.

Also some very special people: The late Diana, Princess of Wales, The Duchess of York, Her Majesty's Ambassador to Tirana Mr. Stephen Nash, David Bicker, Vice Consul British Embassy, Tirana, Max Griggs, Stephen Griggs, Charles Hutton, Eric Harrison, Brian Hillson, Jed Ford, Denys Salt, Peter Rennie, Barbara Lock, George Ridley, Dr. John Maynard, John McGough, The Sisters of The Missionaries of Charity, George Mills, Peter Troy, Val Pridham, Brian Thornton, Jim Suthering, Esther Rantzen, Ken Stones, Norman Wisdom, John Arthur, Jill Trethowan for her kind permission to include the section on Mary Edith Durham, Doce Kruger, Dr. Nicholas Jacobs, Jennie Linden, Phyl Fennelly and finally my wife Jane who has 'been there for me' during the difficult times, and my two sons Haydn and Mansel.

The author extends his gratitude to the authors of *Faith and Compassion* and their publishers, Element Books Ltd. for the reproduction of photographs and Harper Collins publishers for permission to use the extract from *'Something Beautiful For God'*.

Special thanks go to the directors of White Crescent Press Ltd., Rodney Gutteridge, Peter White and John Locke and their superb staff together with 'Task Force Albania's Honorary Secretary Irene Leslie for all her hard work and dedication to the cause.

The author, editor and publisher have made every effort to secure permission to reproduce material protected by copyright. If there are any omissions or oversights, the author, editor and publisher apologise and will make suitable acknowledgements in future printings of this book.

ISBN 0-9517660-8-2

Published by John van Weenen, The Priory, Wollaston, Northamptonshire, England, NN29 7SL.
Tel: 01933 663725
Fax: 01933 664677

Distributed by Biblios Publishers Distribution Services Ltd., Star Road, Partridge Green, West Sussex, England RH13 8LD.
Tel: 01403 710971
Fax: 01403 711143.

Printed by White Crescent Press Ltd., Crescent Road, Luton, Bedfordshire, England LU2 0AG.
Tel: 01582 723122
Fax: 01582 723126.

"Everybody dies – not everybody really lives."

I DEDICATE THIS BOOK TO THE MEMORY OF

JESSICA NEXHIPI

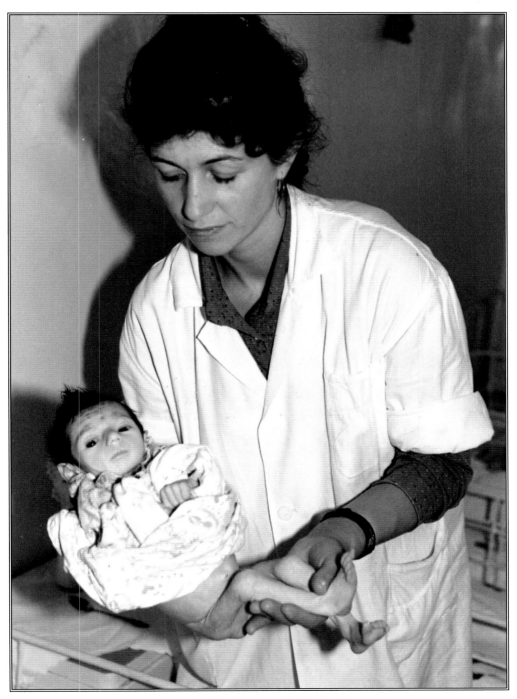

1991 – 1991

ABOUT THE AUTHOR

J ohn van Weenen was born in 1941 and spent his early years in Enfield, Middlesex, United Kingdom.

In 1963, he emigrated to Australia and it was there he became involved in the martial art of karate, which he has practised and taught for thirty-four years.

During his three year stay in the city of Adelaide, John became a volunteer worker for the 'Good Neighbour Council', where he assisted in the rehabilitation of British migrants and the many associated problems connected with settling in a new environment.

Throughout the 'eighties' he organised a number of successful fund raising swimming events, the proceeds of which benefited Bedfordshire's mentally handicapped children.

In 1990, after discovering that his close friend Eddie Whitcher had been diagnosed as having terminal cancer, John decided to raise much needed funds for the Research Unit at the Royal London Hospital in Whitechapel. One year later, he handed the unit's director, Professor Norman Williams, a cheque for £158,000.

A few months later, in September 1991, Bill Hamilton's first harrowing report from Albania appeared on British television screens. It depicted orphaned children, for years neglected by the state and locked behind bars in isolation.

One particular child, Jessica Nexhipi, who sadly died of malnutrition aged five months, weighing one pound less than when she was born, had such an effect on John, that he departed for Albania immediately.

Seven years later, he has led thirty-one relief missions and safely delivered an estimated £7 million of humanitarian aid to northern and central Albania.

His story is inspirational and worth telling, if only for one aspect alone. It reaffirms the *'importance of the individual'* and reminds us, as we approach the Millennium, that one ordinary person can *still* make a difference.

INTRODUCTION

T ime and time again I have been asked the question – why Albania?

Many people have been quick to make the point there are numerous worthwhile causes here in Great Britain that need supporting and after all, shouldn't charity begin at home?

Ironically, when I first learned of Albania's plight, like most British people, I had no idea where the country was. I assumed it could be found in the Middle East or perhaps even further afield. When I finally discovered just how close it was to the UK, it was indeed difficult to comprehend.

How could a country, in 1991, within the confines of Europe, be so incredibly poor? Was it conceivable that a Third World state could exist so close to the relative affluence of Greece and on the very doorstep of Italy.

At that time, I knew nothing of the previous forty-seven years, when the restrictive bonds of communism had virtually strangled the lifeblood out of the Albanian nation.

I was totally ignorant of the hardship and the torture instigated by the 'sigurimi' – Albania's secret police. I knew nothing of the atrocities and the ordeal of political prisoners, destined to spend years in confinement for doing little more than verbally opposing the regime.

That was soon to change and an image lasting 2·8 seconds on BBC Television would be the catalyst for, and the embryo to the forming of 'Task Force Albania'.

Within four months, the largest single convoy of humanitarian aid since World War II, would leave Britain for Albania and in the years ahead, many would follow in its wake.

That story and that of the small group of dedicated volunteers who 'shared my dream' and helped turn it into reality, is told here in the following pages.

John van Weenen
August 1998

North Albanian Alps
2,693 m
8,835 ft

Fierzë
Drin

Shkodër

Kukës

Buenë

Drin

Lezhë

2,246 m
7,369 ft
Dibrë

Milot

Krujë

Mat

✈ AIRPORT

Durrës ✦ **Tirana**

Kavajë

2,257 m
7,405 ft

Albania

Elbasan
RAILROAD Shkumbin

Cërrik Prenjas

Lushnje
OIL FIELD

Pogradec

Seman
OIL PIPELINE

Stalin
Berat
Devoll

Fier

+2,416 m
7,927 ft

Korcë

Ballësh

Selenicë
Osum

Vlorë
Vijosë

Mavrovë
Tepelenë

Strait
of
Otranto

2,486 m
8,156 ft

Gjirokastër
Drin

Lukovë

Finiq

Sarandë

YUGOSLAVIA   ROMANIA
45°   Belgrade ★
An estimated 1,500,000
ethnic Albanians live
in Yugoslavia.
★ Rome
ITALY
Adriatic Sea
ALBANIA
BULGARIA
40°
15°
Ionian
Sea
GREECE
Athens ★
20°

FOREWORD BY ESTHER RANTZEN

I first met John van Weenen when he won a precious 'Heart of Gold' on the BBC Television programme in 1992. Precious, not for its financial value, but because it is only won by the most outstanding people, nominated by those who know them best for their compassion, dedication and unselfishness.

John is just such a man.

The miracles he has created in Albania – and inspired his colleagues to create – beggar description. Most ordinary mortals would find the terrible conditions afflicting Albania's children, particularly the orphans and disabled children, so painful that we would turn aside, intimidated by the sheer size of the problem. But from the moment John saw BBC newsfilm of a baby girl dying of starvation, he decided to do something about it.

This book is the story of the many, many achievements of John and his team, in their hugely difficult struggle to ease the suffering in Albania.

Recently I interviewed John again, on the BBC talk show 'Esther', this time as an example of how much difference one individual can make against enormous odds.

I believe you will find this book a positive inspiration – as indeed John himself has been to all of us.

Esther Rantzen

PREFACE

Albania is a country in south eastern Europe, bounded to the north by Montenegro, to the east by the former Yugoslav Republic of Macedonia, to the south by Greece, and to the west and south west by the Adriatic sea.

Government

Albania has a single-chamber legislature, and a one hundred and fifty-five member People's Assembly. It is elected every four years by universal suffrage by means of the two-ballot majority vote system. An executive president, who is also commander-in-chief of the armed forces and who is debarred from concurrently holding party office, is elected by the People's Assembly. A Prime Minister and council of ministers (cabinet), drawn from the majority grouping within the assembly, has day-to-day charge of government. Private property, freedom of worship and expression, and political pluralism are endorsed by the interim constitution.

History

In the ancient world the area was occupied by the Illyrians, later becoming a Roman province until the end of the 4th century AD. Albania then came under Byzantine rule, which lasted until 1347. There followed about one hundred years of invasions by Bulgarians, Serbs, Venetians, and finally Turks, who arrived in 1385 and, after the death of the nationalist leader Skanderbeg (Georges Kastrioti) (1403-1468), Albania became part of the Ottoman Empire after the siege of Scutari (Shkodra)1478.

Independence

Albania became independent in 1912, after the First Balkan War, and a republic in 1925. In 1928 President Ahmed Beg Zogu was proclaimed King Zog. Overrun by Italy and Germany in 1939-44, Albania became a republic with a communist government in 1946 after a guerrilla struggle led by Enver Hoxha (pronounced: Hodja).

CONTENTS:

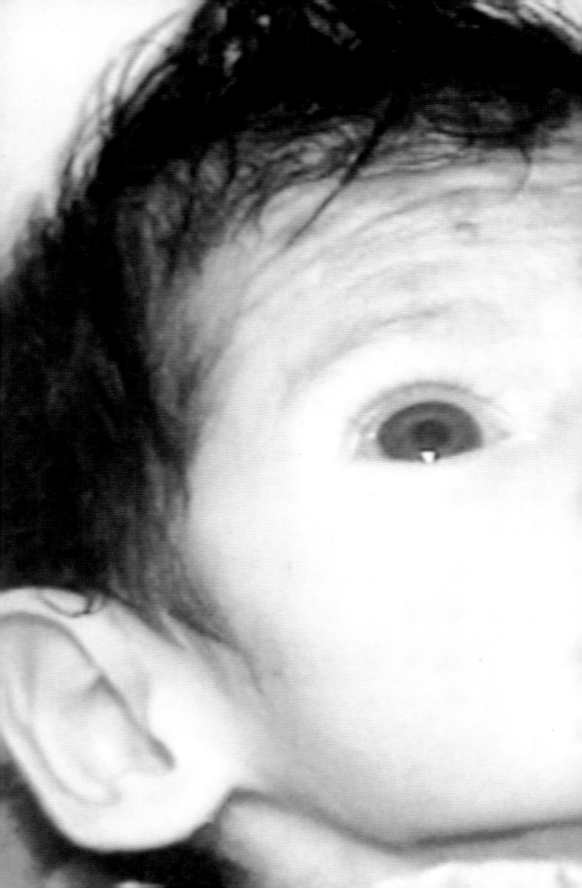

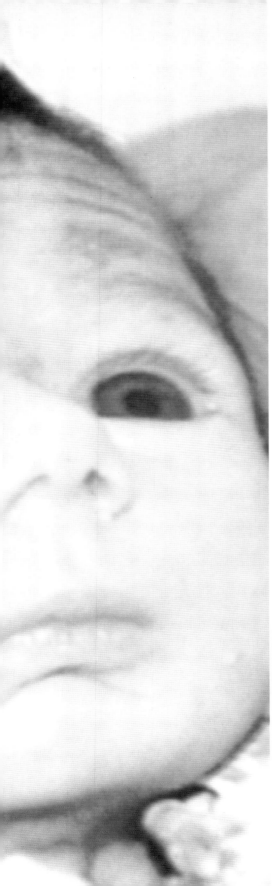

1
JESSICA

A t 7.30 a.m. on 21st September 1991 I awoke and as usual came downstairs and put the kettle on the Aga to make an early morning cup of tea. Stretching across the kitchen cabinet I switched on the television and tuned it to BBC Breakfast News. Still half asleep I found myself gazing at the image of a baby girl on the screen. I have since discovered that the duration of that brief appearance lasted for 2·8 seconds – then she was gone. The kettle boiled and as I poured the water on to the tea bags I thought, "More Romanian children, will it never end?"

During the preceding three or four months, Britain like most western countries had been bombarded with horror pictures following the overthrow of the Ceaucescu regime in Romania. Western journalists had gone in *en masse* and the atrocious conditions they found were graphically illustrated in the pictures they sent back. Within days every television station and every newspaper revealed the unforgettable sights of doors being prised open in dungeon type buildings, only to expose cowering children wallowing in their own excreta, alone, frightened and abandoned.

Naturally, I assumed the nation was being treated to 'more of the same' but the image of that baby girl somehow seemed so much more poignant. Taking the tea bags out, I poured in the milk in appropriate quantities. It was as I picked up the teaspoon I heard the word 'Albania'. "Good Lord" I thought it's happening everywhere and now Albania wherever that is. I stared at the two cups of tea. Somehow they had lost much of their importance. "My God – that poor baby Albanian girl – I must do something – but what?"

Looking up, I was just in time to see the closing pictures of Bill Hamilton's first traumatic report. Indeed it was that report that alerted the world to the suffering taking place in the tiny Balkan state.

In time, Bill would go back to Albania twenty times, committing the journalist's cardinal sin of becoming emotionally involved in a story. Having said that, in doing so, his words came from the heart and his coverage of the struggle by ordinary Albanians to break loose from the bonds of Communism have now won him much acclaim in the world of journalism. Without doubt, Bill Hamilton is a very remarkable person. Deeply religious, he cares for his fellow man and frequently at charity gatherings, when praise is heaped upon him, he dismisses it entirely, claiming only to be "the bearer of the message" and insists it is other people who deserve all the credit.

In 1992 he wrote the book *Albania Who Cares?* and generously devoted a whole chapter to Task Force Albania, so let us take up the story in Bill Hamilton's words . . .

The picture that was to haunt him for a whole month centred on the desperate existence of baby Jessica. Badly malnourished she lay helpless in a rusted cot weighing at age five months, a pound less than when she was born.

I remember her well. A doctor had beckoned me to her bedside after I detected the faint cry of a tiny baby in obvious pain. He picked her up, her entire emaciated body resting in the cradle of his hand.

There was nothing that could be done. Within days Jessica was dead. In the hospital you could sense a feeling of overwhelming relief that her painful, yet eventful life was over without further affliction.

For four days Jessica had been crammed with ten thousand other Albanian refugees on a rusting freighter as her parents made a further bid to flee to the West, but the Italians – overwhelmed by the sheer size of the exodus – had sent them back.

Arben and Mimoza Nexhipi had resumed their wretched lives in a squalid room in the Adriatic port of Durres. They married in their teens and have two other children. Mimoza feels a sense of guilt over Jessica's death, but says that for days the family had nothing to eat, only rags on their backs, and not a Lek* in their pockets to buy a bottle of water for

*Lek is the Albanian currency so named after Prince Leka, the son of the self-proclaimed King Zog.

the terrifying voyage. Mimoza has never worked, Arben lost his job when he developed tuberculosis. They depend on charity to survive.

It would have been easy for van Weenen to sit back, shrug his shoulders and do nothing. Many faced with such horrors on television news bulletins, feel totally inadequate, unable to respond in any meaningful way. What can any individual do in such circumstances that can make any tangible difference? Some sink into the depths of despair, others stretch for handbag or wallet to make a financial contribution. Most, conditioned to scenes of hunger and suffering, mutter a word or two of sympathy and take things no further, preferring to busy themselves in whatever pressing engagements lie ahead on the given day.

What then was to be done? That evening, as he joined friends for dinner, van Weenen had a troubled conscience. Unable to eat anything put in front of him, his mind was already formulating the plan for a staggering humanitarian aid operation.

Van Weenen had two factors in his favour, he had a personal understanding of the real meaning of suffering and an organization behind him whose efforts he could motivate to maximum advantage.

Albania was a country he knew absolutely nothing about. It lay two thousand miles away on the other side of Europe, 'a kind of forbidden land isolated from everywhere and everybody'. Yet that baby had left a marked impression, 'a pathetic little figure, so forlorn and in such obvious pain, it was almost as if she knew she was doomed'.

It was to be another month before things began to fall into place. Van Weenen lives in the adjoining constituency to Prime Minister John Major's Huntingdon seat and he accepted an invitation to attend the Conservative Party Conference at Blackpool.

He had previously been involved in Conservative Party activities in mid-Bedfordshire several years before but nothing since. That was however until the invitation to Blackpool in October 1991. The Winter Gardens were filled to capacity for Mrs. Thatcher's first appearance on the platform since her departure from Downing Street. She rose to speak, emphasized the need for help for the emerging democracies of eastern Europe and told delegates there was someone she wished to introduce. Turning to a tall dark haired man sitting near the edge of the platform, she announced, "This is Dr. Sali Berisha, leader of the Democratic Party of Albania." The delegates rose to their feet and gave him a standing ovation that was clearly exceptional both in its sincerity and its intensity.

Providence had lent the very hand John van Weenen had been looking for. In an instant he knew it. "This is the man I have to talk to – perhaps this is the reason why I came to Blackpool."

Then consternation. As Berisha left the dais, the vast security network that surrounded the platform party prevented van Weenen from getting

*The 'VLORA' docks at Brindisi Harbour in southern Italy in
September 1991 after a desperate two day voyage from the
Albanian port of Durres. On board were ten thousand refugees
boarded together in a frantic bid to flee to the West.
Most were refused entry into Italy and the freighter was sent
back to Durres. Its human cargo was to follow within days.*

anywhere within reach. It took him two days to track Berisha down and finally a leading Conservative Party figure had told him to be in the lobby of the Pembroke Hotel at 11 a.m. Van Weenen pushed his way past the security guards and running up to Berisha he exclaimed, "I simply must speak to you; I have got trucks and aid to bring to Albania."

"Will four o'clock be OK" came the reply.

At four o'clock van Weenen was pacing up and down in the lobby, but Berisha wasn't there. Then suddenly the hotel doors swung open and an unmistakable figure came in, breathless and apologetic. Glancing nervously at his watch he said, "Mr. van Weenen, I'm sorry I'm late, it's two minutes past four".

"Actually I was in a meeting with Mrs. Thatcher and I broke it off to come and see you." Van Weenen felt a little awkward. "You shouldn't have done that, I'm just an ordinary chap." Berisha looked straight into van Weenen's eyes. "Mr. van Weenen – so am I."

Cynical observers might have viewed it as an astute political retort, but somehow van Weenen felt a sense of heartfelt sincerity. The bond of friendship between the karate teacher and the future President of Albania was already being forged.

Conclusion of excerpt from Albania Who Cares?

The story is now taken up by the author:

We sat down in two very plush chairs and I began to tell Dr. Berisha what I had in mind. "I understand many of your people are starving to death. My aim is to bring one or two large trucks to your country loaded with food, but in order to do this, I need to ask you some questions first."

"Please," came the answer.

"How should I come? Which route should I take? Do I need a visa? What about the war in Serbia?"

Dr. Berisha could not answer any of these questions. I sensed his acute embarrassment. This was his first visit to Britain; possibly his first outside Albania. He was a doctor of medicine, a cardiologist. What could he be expected to know about trucking across Europe and such things. "If you really want to help my country," said Dr. Berisha, "then I think you should come and see it first."

With that, he gave me his home telephone number and asked me to call him with details of when I was coming. "I'll help you all I can," said Dr. Berisha, and with that we shook hands and he disappeared into the elevator.

As I caught a taxi back to the Winter Gardens for the last debate of the afternoon, my mind was elsewhere. That old Chinese proverb came to mind, 'A journey of a thousand miles begins with the first step'. I was experiencing mixed emotions, trepidation, fear, excitement, but above all the chance to be able to do something for someone else. My father's words came back to me: "the opportunity of a lifetime can only be taken during the lifetime of the opportunity." I knew that in meeting Dr. Berisha I had taken that first step. Where it would lead me was not important, I just knew it was right. This was my opportunity to 'do something' to help.

"By God, I was going – I was going to Albania!"

"Land of Albania, where Iskander rose,
Theme of the young and beacon of the wise,
And he his namesake, whose oft-baffled foes
Shrunk from his deeds of chivalrous emprize.
Land of Albania, let me bend mine eyes
On thee, thou rugged Nurse of savage men."

'Childe Harold's Pilgrimage'
Lord Byron.

The monument in Skanderbeg Square dedicated to Albania's national hero, Georges Kastrioti Skanderbeg.

2
THE VISIT

Where do I begin? That was the question I posed for myself. The quickest way, or so I thought, was to make a few phone calls. I dialled directory enquiries. "The Albanian Embassy in London, please." "I'm sorry sir, there's no such name listed." I tried again. "OK then, the Albanian Consulate?" – "Nothing for that either sir." Once more " Do you have Albanian anything listed?" – "Nothing sir," came the answer. "What about the Foreign Office in London?" I asked. There was a pause and then the operator said, "You're in luck sir, I've got that one." "Are you sure operator?" – "There's no doubt about it."

The Foreign Office were as helpful as they could be. At that time, the British Government had no official standing or recognition in Albania. There was no ambassador, embassy, consulate or chargé d'affaires in Tirana, Albania's capital. Any contact had to be made through the British Embassy in Rome, but that wasn't very often, as President Ramiz Alia's party of Labour weren't in the least communicative.

"I am sorry I cannot help you further. Incidently have you spoken to Denys Salt at the Anglo-Albanian Association here in London?" It was the best help they could offer.

When I did, Denys couldn't have been more helpful, giving me countless snippets of information. He suggested my notion to take trucks to Albania via Yugoslavia, although admirable, might prove a shade 'risky.' With hindsight – *he couldn't have said a truer word.*

In October 1991, there were two airlines flying to Tirana – Alitalia via Rome and Swiss Air, who had three scheduled flights a week via Zurich. Regent Holidays in Bristol handled most of Swiss Air's charter flights and a return ticket could be bought from them for £240 providing the passenger spent a Saturday night in Albania. At 4.00 a.m. on Monday 21st October, I left my home in Northamptonshire and headed for Heathrow's Terminal Two, but not before faxing Dr. Berisha at the Albanian Democratic Party's headquarters to let him know I was going.

The 8.10 a.m. flight to Zurich was full of businessmen on routine trips to Switzerland but somehow I didn't quite fit in. On the second leg of the trip, there were three passengers apart from myself. Barry Lewis, the acclaimed Sunday Times photographer, together with his journalist partner and a German missionary who planned to disappear into the Albanian Alps with a message that despite the former dictator Enver Hoxha's efforts to 'abolish God' and replace him with unadulterated communism, the plan had misfired and Christianity had survived.

The atmosphere on board the aircraft as it took off from Zurich on the one and a half hour flight to Tirana was a little 'spooky' to say the least. Just imagine, a Swiss Air Fokker 100 cruising at high altitude, virtually empty, save for four isolated passengers. One hoped to spread the word, whilst the second hoped to write it. The third chose to tell his story pictorially leaving myself, in a moment of gross stupidity believing I could save the entire country.

It felt like one of those old 1950s' science fiction films – The Twilight Zone – all four playing out some predestined role, heading into the unknown, into a time warp that had imprisoned Albania for close on fifty years. A voice came over the tannoy system "Ladies and Gentlemen" (there weren't any ladies), "this is your captain speaking, we shall shortly be landing at Tirana International Airport," (that remark should have set alarm bells ringing). "Kindly fasten your seat belts and extinguish any cigarettes – have a nice day".

I am not sure when I realised something was wrong, but something was. Flying down the east coast of Italy avoiding Yugoslavian air space completely, the aircraft had crossed the Adriatic near Bari, circled the Albanian coastline not far from Vlora and begun the final approach to Tirana Airport, by which time, one could make out women in the fields, tilling the land. There was just one problem. The aircraft had not slowed down and I estimated we were still travelling at between three hundred and four hundred miles per hour. I could see the runway ahead – my God – we'll never make it!

Moments later, there were sheep running everywhere and I realised the runway had been covered in them. They were grazing on the strips of grass growing between the large sections of concrete, it was like watching wildebeest scattering across the savannah. Climbing and circling, the pilot brought the plane in for the 'real' landing and soon, we were bumping our way along the landing strip to an eventual halt. The journalists shook their heads, one writing furiously. I breathed a sigh of relief – the missionary let go of his cross. We had arrived in Shqiperi (Albania) – Land of the Eagles.

At that time there were about five landings a week, very rarely two on the same day. Consequently there was great excitement as we disembarked and walked the one hundred yards or so along the tree lined avenue to the airport main building.

It was utter confusion, the airport staff consisting of a complement of two, couldn't cope with the influx of passengers. Four people arriving at the same time, was something of a record. We were shown into a small room, which turned out to be the Immigration Hall and one at a time were dealt with by a customs man, who was very proud and anxious to show off his home-made 'passport stamping machine.'

Ten minutes later the luggage arrived, all four cases of it, on a 'cart affair' towed by a wonderful antiquated Ferguson T20 tractor. Then on, through a door and out into the open. Dr. Berisha came over. "Welcome to Albania" he said and kissed me on both cheeks. I turned to introduce Barry and Ian but they were nowhere to be seen. "Mr. van Weenen, I will see you later. This man will take care of you – goodbye. I have made all the arrangements."

With that, he was gone and I felt just a shade vulnerable. The man in charge whose name was Cuk Vilo ushered me into the back of the strangest vehicle I had ever seen, along with about ten other people. It was a very tight squeeze – my suitcase was somewhere and I turned to the person on my left. "Hello," she said, "I'm Rozi, you're John aren't you?" The girl was strangely beautiful with long wavy black hair and deep green eyes and spoke excellent English. It appeared she had been brought in by Dr. Berisha from the Italian aid agency 'Caritas' to act as my interpreter for the duration of my stay.

Rozi Prekalori

On the forty five minute 'drive' to Tirana, I saw only one other car amidst the hundreds of donkeys, cows and horses and carts. Every two hundred yards or so were shepherds with their tiny flocks of sheep. Tirana had just two hotels, the Dajti and the Tirana. A room had been reserved at the Tirana Hotel and after booking in, which without Rozi would have been a nightmare, I deposited my luggage in the room and she escorted me on my first walkabout of the city.

It was like no other experience I have ever had. There were no cars on the roads, apparently only members of the ruling politburo were allowed cars, and people, unless they had a horse or donkey to ride on, walked everywhere. What bicycles there were, were falling apart and beggar children abounded.

The Tirana Hotel was in Skanderbeg Square, named after the Albanian national hero, Georges Kastrioti Skanderbeg, who led a successful revolt for over twenty five years against the invading Ottoman Turks. I had seen communist countries before, but this was different. There was a distinct air of oppression pervading. People just 'hung around' with nothing to do and nowhere to go.

The country's infrastructure was in tatters and ninety per cent of people were unemployed. The railway network had to be closed down

Skanderbeg Square in Tirana in 1991 when only members of the Politburo and other senior government officials were allowed to own cars

completely because people stole the sleepers for firewood and signalling wire had been torn down to be used in an innovative way to connect street lighting to their homes. There were no raw materials; factory machines stood idle.

Lethargy was setting in and Albanians were losing their desire to work. Soon they would become almost totally dependent on western aid. In the first free elections the Democratic Party had won the cities but lost the rural areas where the country people were much slower to change.

The Government was only to last another three months, to be replaced by an uneasy coalition and that in turn would fail, preparing the way for a Democratic landslide six months later in March 1992.

I made my way back to the hotel where Rozi left me but not before informing me that Dr. Berisha would meet me that evening at 7.00 p.m. in the hotel lobby. We would be having dinner at his house and I looked forward very much to seeing him again.

At 6.45 p.m. I made my way downstairs to the hotel reception. It was dimly lit with small groups of people standing talking to each other. They were mainly journalists and aid workers. I spoke briefly to a representative from the British charity 'Feed The Children' and to some people from 'Médécins Sans Frontières'.

Violence was beginning to erupt here and there and a general feeling of unrest and uncertainty lay just beneath the surface. The water supply to the city had failed and sewerage was becoming a problem. No shops existed, only the daily Tirana market which was fast being transformed into a 'black market' as food became scarcer.

Just after 7.00 p.m. Dr. Berisha arrived. He had acquired a Range Rover which he drove himself, and our first stop was to collect a young American woman working in Tirana and a friend of the Berisha family.

It had been raining hard but had stopped as we threaded our way through the Tirana back streets. I hadn't a clue where we were but I detected a slight urgency in Dr. Berisha's demeanour that the sooner we got to his apartment, the better. Within minutes we had arrived at a sprawling tenement block. His flat was on the first floor and the steps leading to it were ten yards away. As we drove in, the headlight beam picked up a large puddle of water. Dr. Berisha left the car first and we quickly followed suit. As our feet touched the ground they sank in twelve inches of water. It was pitch black and the whole area was flooded. Dr. Berisha didn't know the extent of the flooding and was clearly embarrassed as all three of us waded in the general direction of the steps.

Squelching our way up the stairs we were met by an even more embarrassed Mrs. Berisha and her two children Argita and Shkelzen. To add to the chaos there had been a power failure and Mrs. Berisha who was also a doctor stood with candle in hand like some latter day Florence

Nightingale. We took off our shoes and socks, tipped the water away and wringing our trouser bottoms out, rolled them up to our knees in a somewhat undignified fashion. Minutes later, dry socks and slippers arrived together with the best glass of 'Raki' (distilled wine) I have ever had.

The Berishas' hospitality was overwhelming. They gave everything; nothing was too much trouble. As the evening progressed Dr. Berisha kept us enthralled during dinner and afterwards with his many stories of hardship, suffering and finally resistance to the communist regime. Without doubt he was the country's leading cardiologist having written many papers on the subject and had them published internationally. He lectured at Tirana University regularly and the students held him in high esteem.

With rebellion in the wind, the students had turned to their lecturer, the only man they could trust to carry the banner and put their case to Ramiz Alia and the Politburo for freedom and democracy. Fearing for their safety, as the army had been called in to stamp out these cries for a democratic process, Sali Berisha took their case to the President. It was a brave action, for in preventing much undoubted bloodshed and many students being shot, he put his own life in danger.

Before long, he became the people's choice and was elected as leader of the Albanian Democratic Party. Fate had taken a hand and the forty-eight year old cardiologist was destined for a place in history.

It was about 11.30 p.m. when I was taken back to the Tirana Hotel. The city was deserted. I hadn't seen a soul on the streets – it should have registered – but it didn't. There were no pubs, no restaurants, no discos, in fact, no entertainment of any kind. The hotel reception area was like a morgue and I thought the sooner I got to my room the better. I took a chance and got in the lift. At the third floor I got out, walked a little way along the dingy corridor and into my room. I locked the door and walked over to the window. The city lay asleep, in complete darkness except for the occasional light or two around Skanderbeg Square.

There was no telephone or television in the room, but to my sheer delight there was an old valve radio set on the bedside cabinet. After plugging it in to the mains I was even more surprised when it lit up. Finding the long wave band I began to search for something acceptable, however the atmospherics were so great it appeared very little was getting through. Suddenly a man's voice came through loud and clear: "Good evening, this is the World Service of the BBC from London, here is a summary of the news" . . .

I was ecstatic. Moral reinforcements from Portland Place. I knew that voice – he knew where I was and was speaking to me personally. Well done Auntie – God it's good to be British!

Undressing, I decided not to wash. There was no water anyway, so I cleaned my teeth with some Coca-Cola and settled down into bed to listen to the remainder of the news. I fell sound asleep.

I awoke some time later to the sound of 'gunfire'. I sat bolt upright in bed. After a few seconds I realised I was neither dreaming nor having a nightmare. To my astonishment there really was a gunfight taking place and they weren't hand guns being fired, but automatic rifles.

The window sill was about three foot six inches high and making sure to keep my body below that level, peering out of the window I could see nothing. It was very dark indeed and I quickly decided discretion was the better part of valour.

The Tirana Hotel was the tallest building in Tirana and could easily become a target for some 'trigger happy' gunman. That being the case I carefully pulled the mattress off the bed complete with sheets and blankets and on to the floor, and that's where I stayed, below window sill height, until 8.30 next morning.

In the two days that followed I was provided with a car, a driver and Rozi, my interpreter. I saw most of what I had come to see. Tirana's three main hospitals were pitiful. Conditions there were beyond belief. There was no bottled oxygen available as the factory that produced it in the past had closed down. Each ward had only a handful of syringes, and with neither sterilizing equipment available nor hot water, each syringe was used time and time again. The risk of cross infection was enormous.

Blood transfusions and drips were controlled by hair clips on the line, toilet facilities were non-existent, nothing more in most cases than a crude hole in the ground. Beds were rusted and broken, sheets and blankets, where they existed, were torn, filthy and bloodstained. The overall internal condition of the wards was beyond belief. Dankness pervaded everywhere caused by the crumbling plaster and fallen masonry that was obviously responsible for most of the walls being covered in mould. The hospital wards were nothing more than a shell lined on either side by rusty beds. The despondency on the patients' faces was almost matched by that of the nurses. Telling the difference between a patient and a nurse was not always that easy. However, a rule of thumb seemed to be that the patients were the bandaged horizontal people whilst the nurses were vertical and often mobile. Apart from that they were virtually indistinguishable.

I had seen enough. I couldn't stay there any longer. The chaos, the confusion, the disorganisation of everything was too much to take. Although I didn't know it at the time, I was in the initial stages of what has now become known as 'The Albanian Syndrome,' but more of that later.

It was Thursday and my flight was scheduled for departure at 2.00 p.m. The possibility of boarding the wrong flight was not a problem as the Swiss Air flight was the only one that day.

I said goodbye to Cuk Vilo who had driven me to the airport. "Thank you for everything – I'll be back."

As the Swiss Air jet climbed high into the sky I watched Albania slip away into the afternoon mist. The unfamiliar coastline gave way to the broad expanse of the Adriatic Sea. I looked around the cabin. There were one hundred empty seats, and just three other passengers, each occupying a window seat – in splendid isolation and alone with their thoughts. The aircraft turned and I caught my last glimpse of Shqiperi, Land of the Eagles and then it was gone. I thought of Dr. Berisha's last words to me, "Thank you for coming – we need your help".

In that moment I detected all the hope yet all the sadness in the world in his voice. I knew then what I must do and with God's help – I'd do it.

The author with Dr. Sali Berisha in October 1991

3

THE CONVOY

F rom the outset, one thing was blatantly obvious. *I* needed help almost as much as the people I hoped to assist, for I really had no idea where to start.

Karate was all I knew, but of no use to the Albanians at that juncture. What I did have, was a group of loyal students. Only once before had I asked them for help and that was to raise funds for Professor Norman Williams at the Royal London Hospital in Whitechapel for cancer research. They had responded magnificently, and nine months later as the campaign drew to a close, Professor Williams was handed a cheque for one hundred and fifty eight thousand pounds.

This was a different 'kettle of fish' but I had every confidence they would respond in a positive way. The practice of traditional karate and the doctrines and philosophy of Gichin Funakoshi, the man credited with bringing karate to the Japanese mainland from Okinawa, emphasised the importance of helping people less fortunate than oneself. Indeed, in his autobiography, written just prior to his death in 1957, he wrote the following words:

'Make benevolence your lifelong duty. This surely is an important mission. It is a lifelong effort, truly a long journey.'

Back in England, I contacted the twenty-five karate clubs under my control and chose a representative from each. I then convened a meeting for Sunday 3rd November, 1991 in Bedford, and invited the twenty-five plus any others who were interested. Seventy five people turned up, and I told them the whole story.

Two and a half hours of non stop talking later, every single person in the room pledged their support. They had all seen the TV reports, the mood was right and the timing perfect and so – Task Force Albania ('TFA') was born. The plan was to take one or two juggernaut trucks packed with food to the starving people in the cities of Kavaja and Shkodra which basically presented three problems.

Firstly, how to get enough free food to fill two, thirty-eight tonne trucks. Secondly, how to raise £4,000 to pay for the trucks and thirdly, the trip and distribution. The following extract is taken from *Albania Who Cares?* by kind permission of Bill Hamilton:

Everyone must lend a hand. The idea of helping people in such dire trouble was a noble one, going to the very heart of all they were striving for in the practice of karate.

Specific targets were set, even though van Weenen knew that at this stage they might prove impossible to meet. "On 26 January 1992," he announced, "a convoy of TASK trucks will leave Bedford for Albania loaded with supplies, and the convoy will be accompanied by a support team of karate students. This will require very little time and effort. However, that little effort from everyone is vital to the success of the whole operation."

Van Weenen knew full well it was the understatement of the year.

He had twenty-five karate clubs spread across twenty-five towns, most of them situated in the Midlands and the South. The job now was to entice public involvement as well.

Small advertisements were inserted in the national Press. There was a desperate need for children's clothing, baby food, toys, bed and cot linen and medical supplies. Schoolchildren were asked to approach their headteacher with a view to the school starting a collection. Anyone having contacts with clothing, food or pharmaceutical companies was asked to get in touch with them immediately and plead for assistance.

Would it all be a cry in the dark or were there really people out there anxious and willing to respond to the call? Was this an ego trip or was God the motivator behind it all, spurring him on and urging him to put his undoubted organizational talent to maximum use? These were the questions that lay heavily on van Weenen's mind.

The plan was simple and straightforward.

Bedford would serve as the headquarters for the whole operation. From this wheel hub – twenty-five spokes would project out – each of them leading to one of the twenty-five towns where his karate clubs were located. On top of all this, he envisaged at least another one hundred cities and towns becoming involved through the initial efforts of just one volunteer.

The concept worked almost to the letter. Within minutes of his advertisement appearing, the telephone at 'Fineshade', his Northamptonshire home, began to ring incessantly. The first caller from Edinburgh. A box of babies nappies – where should they be sent?

Van Weenen listened politely. "Thank you. Now would you do something more for me? If you really want to help, there is something I would ask you to undertake right away. Pop down to your local newspaper, tell the editor you're collecting for Task Force Albania, mention your address and ask him to put a few lines in next week's edition. You'll be surprised how many people will want to help."

A few days later and callers were back on the line. Van Weenen could sense the desperation – even panic – this time. "We simply can't cope. Our homes are full. My husband's complaining he can't get into the bathroom. My children are tripping up all over the place, there's just so much stuff. You'll have to bail me out!"

Van Weenen was prepared. "You'll have to get on to your priest or minister. Get him to give you a church hall or try the school or the local council. They'll find you somewhere."

The convoy in Yugoslavia.

Within a couple of weeks, another frantic call: "The vicar wants the hall emptied . . . the school says we'll have to get out, they've cancelled PE lessons because the gymnasium is jammed to the roof. How are we to get all the bags to you?"

The job was now to remain absolutely calm; "Pop down to the paper again. Get them to print another paragraph or two asking if there's anyone out there with a truck who would be willing to collect and bring everything to Bedford. You'll be surprised at the response. Lots of people have been waiting for such an opportunity . . . they just don't know how to go about it."

Soon a vast array of pantechnicons were weaving their way across country lanes on to the M1 en route for Bedford. Van Weenen's initial belief was that he would fill two trucks. The evidence told a very different story. Over seven hundred and forty tons of food, clothes and medicines which would fill no fewer that twenty thirty-eight tonne trucks, and so far the entire operation had cost not a single penny.

Getting the aid to Albania was an entirely different matter. Evaluating the money that would be required for diesel, ferry fares and documentation, it was decided to hand over to a firm of professional road hauliers. Van Weenen's job now was to raise £1,800 per truck. Given his administrative abilities, that was achieved within days.

The drivers briefing gets underway on board the P & O superferry.

As the target date approached, it became obvious that the existing team of volunteers, even working around the clock, could not sort through, label and pack the vast amount of aid which now occupied half a sprawling industrial estate.

The police, army and even the American Airforce were contacted. Scores of servicemen and police cadets were hurriedly despatched. By day and night the loading continued apace.

The Departure

At precisely two o'clock on Sunday 26th January the Lord Lieutenant of Bedfordshire signalled the trucks on their way. As they swept out of the compound in driving rain to the accompaniment of 'Land of Hope and Glory' booming from the loudspeakers, van Weenen could not have imagined the drama that lay ahead.

He had met the drivers just a couple of hours before. Most were self-employed, a good blend of youth and experience. Though apprehensive of what might be involved, the spirit was one of ebullience.

The convoy extended for a mile as it negotiated its way over the new Dartford Bridge and down the M2 to Dover. The entire top deck of a P & O super ferry was required to transport all the trucks and support vehicles to the Belgian port of Zeebrugge.

On sped the convoy through Germany, Czechoslovakia and into Hungary. Approaching Budapest, van Weenen, fatigued after a nine-hour stint at the wheel, pulled into a service area and asked a freelance cameraman, Tim Eyrl, who was travelling with him in one of the Range Rovers to take over. Eyrl's colleague, Annabel, remained in the back seat.

The Task Force trucks in radio contact had gone ahead. The other support vehicles were behind. As darkness descended, Eyrl pulled out on to the motorway, van Weenan as yet to secure his seatbelt.

The Range Rover filed into the inside lane of the three-lane highway. Within seconds, a dark coloured truck was detected just a few feet in front. It had no lights. Realizing the imminence of a collision, Eyrl swung the wheel violently to the left. At seventy miles an hour the Range Rover went out of control. It careered across all three lanes, hit the central crash barrier and then rebounded into the side of the truck they had vainly tried to overtake. Eyrl had completely lost control and van Weenen could not get to the steering wheel because he was being thrown in all directions as a result of failing to fasten his seat belt in time.

The vehicle slewed again, this time across the centre lane before careering towards the last barrier guarding the motorway from a five hundred feet drop into a wooded ravine. 'Being a tall vehicle van Weenen thought the Range Rover was going to go right over, but it hit the barrier at a slight angle and ricocheted up the hard shoulder before finally coming to a halt. It was a complete write-off. By rights they should have been killed. All their equipment – food, clothes and their plans for the entire journey – had disappeared out of the window and were lost. If ever they needed a signal from the 'Almighty' that he wanted the mission completed, then this was it.'

Within twelve hours the three were able to obtain a replacement car. Dazed, but relatively unscathed, they were on their way to Yugoslavia, having by now lost all contact with the convoy.

The nightmare, though, was far from over. The truck drivers had pulled up at a pre-determined stopping place near Belgrade. Van Weenen arrived there the following day. With midnight approaching and suffering from delayed shock and a grave lack of sleep, all he wanted to do was get straight to bed.

Two of his karate students intervened. They were sorry, they said, but he faced enormous problems. "There's a mutiny in the camp. The truck drivers have decided to call it a day." Getting closer to the Albanian border they were feeling decidedly unhappy. One had been in touch with his wife who told him a trucker had been killed and that vehicles were being attacked and ransacked. Some were getting panicky... and they had been drinking. These were professional truck drivers and they wanted a meeting that minute. Van Weenen's team said they would come in too, but he feared that would cause a confrontation and given the state that some of the drivers were in, they would have been annihilated if it had come to blows.

There was nothing else for it. Van Weenen went into the room alone.

For five and a half hours he was subjected to a barrage of angry protests. Then he addressed every complaint in turn until at last tempers began to cool and the truckers shook hands in an obvious display of reassurance. They were an essential part of the team and as such would be properly looked after. But John had another twenty men to wet nurse and they were a very big problem at the time. It had been another close shave for van Weenen, but his faith in his venture had still not wavered.

Despite the war in Serbia, the convoy experienced no problems, but crossing into Macedonia they ran into deep snowdrifts. Many of the mountain passes were virtually impassable. Chaos ensued as trucks began to lose their grip on the treacherous surface. Some slid off the road and into a ditch. Van Weenen urged the drivers to attach chains to their tyres only to be told that they hadn't brought any. In Skopje, a blacksmith was pressed into service to provide a dozen pairs and the push continued towards Albania.

At the border everything again came to a standstill. Such was the disorganisation of the Albanian guards that it took fourteen hours of cajoling before the convoy was allowed in.

On through the polluted industrial city of Elbasan and darkness was descending as the party arrived at an important crossroads. Here, eleven of the trucks were scheduled to turn left along the valley to Kavaja, the other nine to be sent across the mountains and on to Tirana and Shkodra.

The team stopped briefly to consult maps and check the listings locating the exact position of the food and medicines on each truck. Within two minutes the cry went up, "We're being attacked." Dozens of people had emerged from the fields, surrounded a number of the trucks and were slashing at the tilt sheets with machetes. The tarpaulins were ripped open and organized teams were rushing to remove the boxes one at a time.

Van Weenen, fearing the worst, ordered his men into the cabs to remove the baseball bats they'd brought along just in case the locals fancied a sporting challenge somewhere along the way. Together, they charged down the road wielding their bats in anger. The ploy worked. Wondering what might come next, the raiders disappeared just as quickly as they had come.

By the time the convoy reached Kavaja, the whole city was in complete darkness. Representatives of the Democratic Party were waiting and the trucks were escorted to an armed warehouse five miles outside the town. Everyone had wanted to deliver straight to the starving townspeople. They were told that this would spark a riot. So the army guarded the load overnight. The next day everything did get through to those in need. Other deliveries would not prove so straightforward.

"One of our Range Rovers is missing".

Parked overnight in Tirana, the nine remaining truck drivers were terrified. In an enclosed compound, they watched in horror as the guards, equipped with their Chinese made rifles, began to help themselves. The pilfering went on for hours. The lights went too.

The drivers were adamant. They would not proceed to Shkodra unless they were given an armed escort. Berisha was contacted and promised to help, but the Democrats' Communist partners in the uneasy Coalition Government would lend no support. For three days the trucks remained in the compound, their drivers refusing to move.

Berisha was called one last time. "Unless you have twelve policemen here by morning, the trucks will smash their way out of these gates and take everything to Romania." At dawn the policemen arrived. Armed guards in every cab and an escort front

Somehow, the convoy had to get over these mountains and without snowchains it was going to be very difficult.

26

A little boy from Kavaja cannot believe his good fortune. He has been given a *whole tin* of sponge pudding.

This blond Albanian boy knows nothing of computers or mountain bikes. Happiness to him is two loaves of bread.

and rear. The police gave a clear instruction – stay tightly packed and do not let anyone break in between you. The convoy left at breakneck speed with horns blaring, traffic lights were crossed at red.

Out into the country, van Weenen noticed a car coming up from behind, its lights flashing. Three times it tried to squeeze its way into the convoy, three times it failed. The drivers had outmanoeuvred the bandits. Half a mile up the road another gang was lying in wait ready to take the spoils should the team have been forced to stop.

In Shkodra the trucks were taken straight to the military compound. It was an explosive situation with the soldiers firing their automatic weapons in the air to create confusion. Discipline had broken down. The soldiers and police were helping themselves. People were arriving from every direction all intent on taking everything on which they could lay their hands. Boxes were disappearing over walls, under fences, through open doors. The desperation of ordinary people flocking to the gates was all too apparent. Old women, their hands pushed through every hole in the barbed wire perimeter, were begging and pleading for every parcel in sight. Unmercifully, the police smashed their hands with truncheons and the butts of their rifles.

Mountain children enjoying a game of ring-a-ring-of-roses for the first time.

In the chaos the equivalent of one truck load was lost, but ninety per cent of the total was successfully locked in the warehouse and later delivered to thousands on the edge of starvation.

Twenty trucks had begun the journey and twenty returned. Fifty men went in, fifty came out. No one was hurt. Under the conditions it was a remarkable achievement.

Within months van Weenen would be back in Albania on a new and even more moving mercy mission. This time his sensitivity and persistence were to lead to blind Albanian orphans – for years neglected by the state and left in misery and degradation – receiving the gift of sight. How it was achieved is the subject of the next chapter in this continuing story of a remarkable human response to those so long deprived of hope, dignity and even the most basic of human rights.

Van Weenen is not in doubt that God's guiding hand played a significant part in his mission.

(Here Bill Hamilton's excerpt ends and the story is once again taken up by the author).

A thief being apprehended by soldiers.

THE SUPPORT TEAM

Looking back now, I am more convinced than ever of what a superb team I had on Task Force Albania's first humanitarian convoy.

Thirty men and women, mostly senior karate students, travelling in seven support vehicles, using their annual holiday and paying all their own expenses. I was very proud of them.

For many, it was their first 'sortie' to a 'third world' country, with all the associated shock and trauma, but I have to say, their application, dedication and loyalty were second to none.

Six years later, many have gone their own way and are spread to the four corners of the earth, but I am sure, in a quiet moment of reflection, all will recall with fond memories, the spirit and camaraderie of a period that was most exciting yet extremely dangerous.

Louise Cooper holding seven year old Nazima at the Kavaja compound.

With hindsight, had we been aware of the dangers, many of us would not have gone, but dealing with problems on a day to day basis became second nature out of necessity. We were always very much a team and the decisions taken were the right ones at the time, regardless of the outcome.

In listing the names of the Support Team, I would like to record a debt of gratitude I owe to each and every one of them.

Alan Blake	Joanna Kettle	John Dawson
Alan Bristow	Steve Thompson	Joanna Snel
Roy Hazelwood	Jacqueline Malam	Gursharan Sahota
Tony Benford	Richard Patterson	Tim Eyrl
Greg Mort	David Fox	Arthur Tooms
Royden Richards	Kim Watson	Carolyne Watson
Vic Kaye	Susan Thorn	Jane Sydenham
Pedro Barker	Carole Barker	Azad Kumar
Annabelle Studholme	Louise Cooper	Stuart Bennett
Stephen Clay	Kevin Burton	

Each member of the team brought his or her own special qualities to bear, but overall gelled into a very tight cohesive group. Alan Blake will be remembered for his quiet but steadying influence in times of trouble, whilst Joanna Kettle, young at the time, grew up amazingly quickly and became most dependable.

I never had any doubts whatsoever about Alan Bristow. Steve Thompson and Joanna Snell were not members of the karate fraternity and therefore exhibited their 'free spirits' initially. However, that situation did not last and they soon became popular and respected by all. Roy Hazelwood was as solid as a rock but then – I expected him to be. Jacqueline Malam, Susan Thorn, Kim and Carolyne Watson, Carole and Pedro Barker and Tony Benford were all great.

I will always remain grateful to Carole Barker for the compassion she showed one black Hungarian night when all was nearly lost and although we have lost touch with each other, I hope she will always think of me as a friend.

Gursharan Sahota was always supportive in every conceivable way, whilst Tim Eyrl and Annabel Studholme were there primarily to do a professional job as 'in house' photographers – and they did.

Greg Mort supplied us with everything we requested, including some of the photographs in this book. We were all delighted when one of his pictures found its way onto the front page of the *Daily Telegraph*.

David Fox and Arthur Tooms were most helpful indeed and in Budapest, Arthur came to my rescue as he did so often in Albania. It was most reassuring to have people like Roy Richards along and Vic Kaye kept us all amused, intrigued, or something like that, with his never ending stories of the Turks and the Ottoman Empire.

Our very own nurse Mrs. Jane Sydenham kept a beady eye on everyone – a first class lady! Azad Kumar came up trumps. It was the first of many trips he would make, and although he has put a great deal in, I feel, like most of us, he has got a great deal more back.

Nurse Jane Sydenham

Finally, young Louise Cooper, who was wonderful with the Albanian children and is now a proud mother herself, and the three lads from Royston, Stuart Bennett, Stephen Clay and their good friend Kevin Burton, all were a great credit to their families – their behaviour throughout was exemplary – which brings me last, but not least to John Dawson.

At that time John worked for BP and although I shall never know how he did it, he managed to persuade BP to give us a lot of assistance for the journey. Without doubt, his major achievement was to get free fuel for all seven support vehicles from BP stations en route, which meant, we got to Albania and back at very little cost.

Whilst on the trip, he played a major supportive role and time and time again, I heeded his wise counsel. He had the ability to sum up a situation, make a decision and proffer a solution but, and this is the great thing – only when asked to do so.

On his return to England, he wrote a concise forty-one point assessment of the trip, seen through his eyes and I thought it well worth including here. His account, as a junior member of the team, may assist the reader in forming a balanced view of the mission and I am most grateful to him for taking the time and trouble to prepare it.

TASK FORCE ALBANIA – STATISTICS/FACTS

"**1. SEPTEMBER 1991** – Sensei* John van Weenen, Chief Instructor of the Traditional Association of Shotokan Karate saw Bill Hamilton's report on the Albanian orphans and decided to do something about it.

The report had said that they were desperate for aid to help them survive the winter.

2. OCTOBER 1991 – Sensei van Weenen met Dr. Sali Berisha the leader of the Albanian Democratic party and got assurances that the Democratic Party would ensure that aid would get to and remain with the people for whom it was intended.

3. Members of the Traditional Association of Shotokan Karate pledged their full support for a campaign to take a convoy of short term aid to Albania and for volunteers, at their own expense, to accompany the aid to see that it got to the right people. The weekend of 25th January was chosen as the departure date.

4. SATURDAY 2ND NOVEMBER 1991 – TASK FORCE ALBANIA was launched, immediately captured the public's imagination and quickly had the makings of the largest single convoy of aid for Albania and the largest convoy ever to leave the UK in peacetime.

5. Sensei van Weenen visited Albania to see at first hand, how best to

*11 year old Shima
finds happiness with
some new friends*

help the poor unfortunate orphans. He targeted the hospital in Kavaja together with the orphanages in Shkodra to receive aid in the form of medicines, medical equipment, food, clothes, toys, beds, and bedding. In addition it was decided that, since there was little if any fuel being distributed in the country, we should gather blankets, clothes and shoes for the men, women, and children of Kavaja and Shkodra.

6. A central warehouse was acquired, fed both directly and via local warehouses organised by clubs in the Association. Many very generous donations, were made by individuals, schools, churches, and industry and it soon became necessary to open a second warehouse.

7. SUNDAY 12TH JANUARY 1992 — The final arrangements were agreed and the volunteers accompanying the convoy confirmed. In addition to members of T.A.S.K. we had a nurse, two voluntary aid workers, a children's nanny, two camera crew, and two independent press photographers.

8. THURSDAY 23RD - SATURDAY 25TH JANUARY 1992 — Hundreds of volunteers, including over one hundred and fifty police cadets from Hendon, loaded the vehicles in record time. Each vehicle had a manifest which logged its contents and its ultimate destination e.g. the mentally handicapped orphanage in Shkodra.

9. SUNDAY 26TH JANUARY 1992 — A very emotional send-off by families, friends, local dignitaries and clergy from police headquarters at Kempston, Bedford. Televison, press and radio had been made aware of the enormity of the event and covered both the loading and the departure of the twenty trucks and seven support vehicles. The police provided a motor cycle escort to the motorway and other forces en route had been asked to give us every assistance (and hopefully, no speeding tickets).

10. MONDAY 27TH JANUARY 1992 — The planned 12.30 a.m. sailing from Dover to Zeebrugge was full, so six hours were immediately lost against schedule. We left Dover at 6.30 a.m. for the four hour crossing – the Channel was as calm as a mill pond. The time was well spent discussing the route and ensuring that we all knew where to rendezvous that evening.

John Williams, the convoy leader had decided that we should not travel as one very large convoy until we reached the Yugoslavian border.

Further delays were experienced as we made our way through Belgium, Germany, Czechoslovakia, Hungary, Yugoslavia, and Albania – due to border delays (despite having the trucks sealed by customs officers at Dover), mechanical problems with the trucks and bad weather from Skopje to Bitola and Lake Ohrid – the four days planned for the outward leg stretched to seven.

11. No contact with the UK was possible for six days from 30th January – (three days before we entered Albania), until the night of

5th February, when we were in the Yugoslavian mountains.

A very nerve-racking time for families and friends especially since there had been reports of an aid vehicle being attacked and local papers carried stories of chaos and confusion.

12. SUNDAY 2ND FEBRUARY 1992 – The final push up the mountain to the Albanian border took all morning and finally the complete convoy was assembled for block clearance through the formalities.

13. As planned, representatives of the Albanian Democratic Party met us at the border with the police escort we had been promised.

They confirmed what we already knew from meetings with the Red Cross and other aid agencies such as Feed The Children and The Adventist Development & Relief Agency (ADRA); that it would be far too dangerous for us to take the aid into the towns – we would draw attention to the very institutions we were trying to help, and make them targets for bandits.

It was agreed that we should take the trucks to guarded compounds and let the Albanian Democrats distribute the aid using local transport and ambulances.

14. Border formalities had taken hours, and darkness was falling as the convoy stretching out for over a mile, crept down the twisting, turning, unlit, poorly surfaced road which fast became treacherous as temperatures dropped to sub zero.

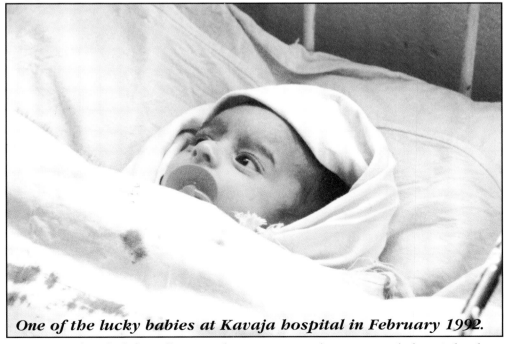

One of the lucky babies at Kavaja hospital in February 1992.

15. We headed for Elbasan where we were due to spend the night, but plans were changed en route and the convoy was divided up: eleven trucks and six support vehicles went directly to Kavaja, and the other nine plus the remaining support vehicle went to Tirana to spend the night in a guarded compound.

16. The Kavaja compound was six or seven kilometres outside the town, in a disused quarry. The local Mayor and the Director of Education were all there to meet us and confirm that they would personally guarantee that the aid would get to the people for whom it was intended.

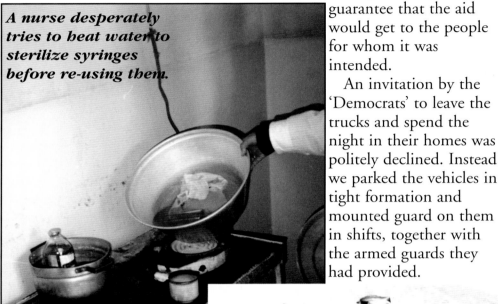

A nurse desperately tries to heat water to sterilize syringes before re-using them.

An invitation by the 'Democrats' to leave the trucks and spend the night in their homes was politely declined. Instead we parked the vehicles in tight formation and mounted guard on them in shifts, together with the armed guards they had provided.

17. MONDAY 3RD FEBRUARY 1992 – At 7.00 a.m., fifty to sixty men appeared out of nowhere and as the morning wore on, more and more arrived to help unload the trucks. By nightfall all eleven vehicles had been unloaded into the magazines inside the compound.

Meanwhile, some of the support team and the camera

Many hands make light work.

crew, visited the hospital in Kavaja to see where much of the aid was destined to go. Already, medicines, baby food, blankets, and incubators from our convoy had arrived at the hospital.

A tour of the hospital followed, and we saw the appalling conditions and totally inadequate medicines and equipment they had to work with. Paper clips were being used to control the flow of drips, there were no sterilisers, no heating, and many doors and windows were broken or missing.

Three of the support vehicles headed off to rendezvous with the nine trucks and support vehicle in Tirana and then made their way to Shkodra.

18. Back at the compound, members of the support team played games with the local children, and the truck drivers joined in the distribution of clothes, (shoes were in very great demand), toys and sweets.

Some of the team, truck drivers and children at the remote Kavaja compound in February 1992.

The joy of giving caused many a moist eye even amongst the hardened men of the world fraternity of truck drivers.

19. The atmosphere was happy and relaxed, the 'Democrats' seemed well organised and very appreciative of our efforts.

The local children reappeared wearing the shoes and clothes we had distributed regardless of whether they fitted or not.

20. At the end of the day, we formed the trucks and support vehicles similar to a wagon train and had an enormous camp fire and fry-up – the feeling of achievement and a job well done was very evident.

The truck drivers thoughts turned to return loads from Greece, Turkey, Bulgaria or Romania.

Receiving her first sweet.

21. TUESDAY 4TH FEBRUARY 1992 – The truck drivers' task completed, we said our farewells to them and the local children (who were still wearing the clothes we had brought). The three remaining support vehicles went back to the hospital in Kavaja, where we saw more evidence of our aid having arrived.

22. We followed the coast road up past Durres and headed north to Shkodra. The landscape was desolate – all the trees had been cut down for fuel, and the pill boxes (over six hundred and fifty thousand of them had been built under communist rule, allegedly to protect the Albanians from invasion), littered the countryside.

23. Eventually, we arrived in Shkodra, and after several false starts, we were taken to the compound in the centre of town, which was already surrounded by crowds of people.

There we met up with the rest of the convoy, and discovered that whilst there seemed to be plenty of armed guards and officials, few workers were in evidence.

24. We set to work unloading the trucks whilst the Albanian officials were harangued about the lack of help. They promised that help was on its way and that the trucks would be unloaded overnight.

25. A visit to the orphanage was organised for us, and the seven support vehicles cautiously threaded their way through the throngs of Albanians wandering

41

*A man sits warming himself by an **unlit** wood burning stove. It's the middle of winter, there is no heating and the windows, patched with polythene sheeting, are wide open.*

aimlessly along the roads.

26. Whilst the orphanage was in a bad state of repair, the children were clean, well clothed and obviously very happy. The staff were dedicated to the children – and the children to them. Each had seven children to care for and worked from 7.00 a.m. till 8.00 p.m. – seven days a week. Little eyes lit up at the toys and sweets we had brought and laughter, cuddles and kisses abounded.

Our hearts went out to these beautiful children, many of whom had sight or hearing problems, but all too soon it was time to leave and a head count was required to ensure that we hadn't smuggled anyone out with us.

An orphan boy finds comfort in the arms of Azad Kumar.

27. Back we went to the compound, where the crowds had grown even larger and help with the unloading was still very scarce. Once more we were assured that more help was on its way, and all the trucks would be unloaded by morning.

28. WEDNESDAY 5TH FEBRUARY 1992 – Morning arrived – and guess what? The storage in the compound was full and there were still two trucks to unload.

29. Local transport and ambulances were arriving and loading up with supplies, but it would have taken a full day or more to create sufficient room for the two truckloads still to be off-loaded.

30. The crowd had grown still larger

Unwanted children sit – and wait.

and was becoming restless as it saw goods being moved out of the compound – people were begging at the compound gates, desperate for the aid we had brought.

31. Heads appeared over the perimeter wall, then bodies were on top of the wall.

A guard standing a few feet from us let off a round of warning shots over the heads of the crowd – the noise was deafening. Moments later, more shots were fired and headlines of people being shot dead in bread queue riots sprang to mind.

32. It was getting very uncomfortable – the truck drivers were extremely tense from the night's activities. (They had slept locked in their cabs whilst the unloading took place.) They wanted out now, and all together. There was safety in numbers, and no-one wanted to be left behind. The drivers realised the crowd meant us no harm, but in their desperation to get to the aid we had brought – albeit much of it being for them – they could cause severe damage to the trucks which were, of course, the drivers' livelihood (and probably not insured in the circumstances).

33. Suggestions that the two trucks still not unloaded could go directly to an outlying village, escorted by the Albanian 'Democrats' were rejected out of hand. The trucks were leaving in half an hour, be they full or empty.

34. The only course of action was to empty their loads onto the

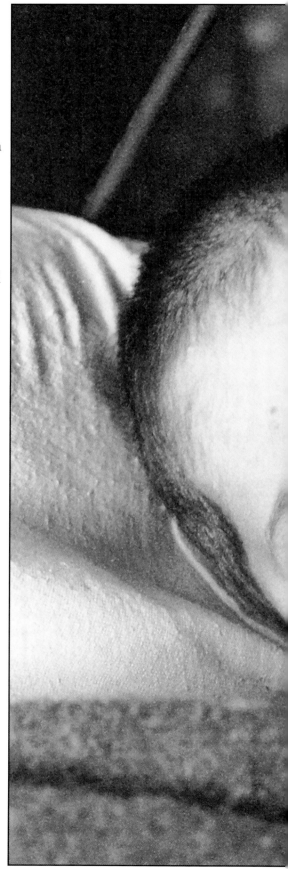

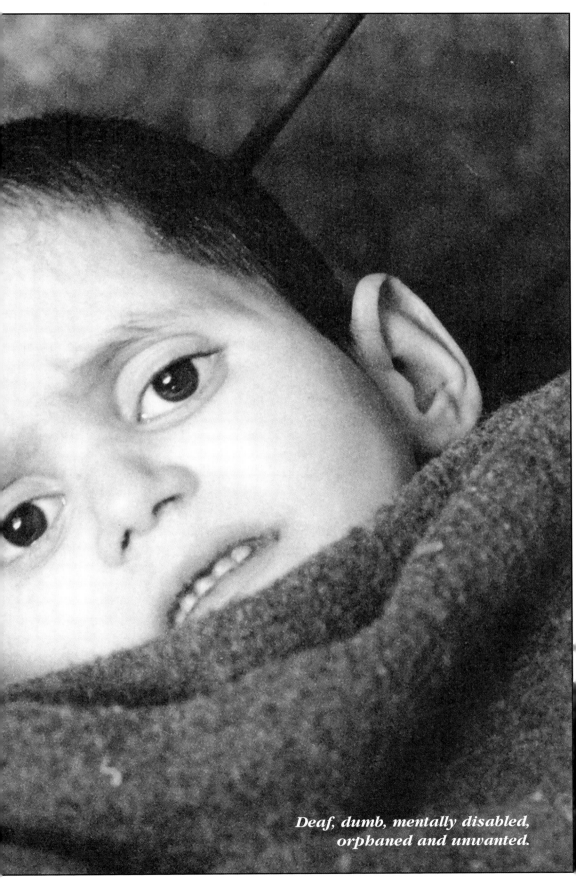

Deaf, dumb, mentally disabled, orphaned and unwanted.

A lonely lice ridden girl peers out of a window at Shkodra's mentally handicapped institute in February 1992.

ground, outside the building as quickly as possible. This, unfortunately, is what independent television chose to show.

35. Once the trucks were safely away, we loaded the support vehicles with medicine, food, and toys and went to the mentally handicapped orphanage, where we were greeted with open arms by doctors, nurses and patients.

We parked inside the walled hospital grounds, but, being in the centre of the town, crowds were gathering even as we closed the gates behind us.

36. Having quickly unloaded the aid, we were shown around the orphanage, which was in a terrible state of repair – broken windows, missing doors, non-existent plumbing, no heating with damp and decay everywhere.

The mentally handicapped children were huddled together in a corner of the room, with bare floors, exactly as Bill Hamilton's report had shown.

Many had shaven heads – the only answer to head lice when there is no medication and the only way to treat the bleeding caused by constant scratching and banging of heads against the walls.

We handed out the toys we had brought, and held, cuddled and played with the children. Their response was immediate, it was obvious they needed someone to touch them, show interest and give them mental stimulation.

37. Unfortunately, we had to cut our visit short – the crowd

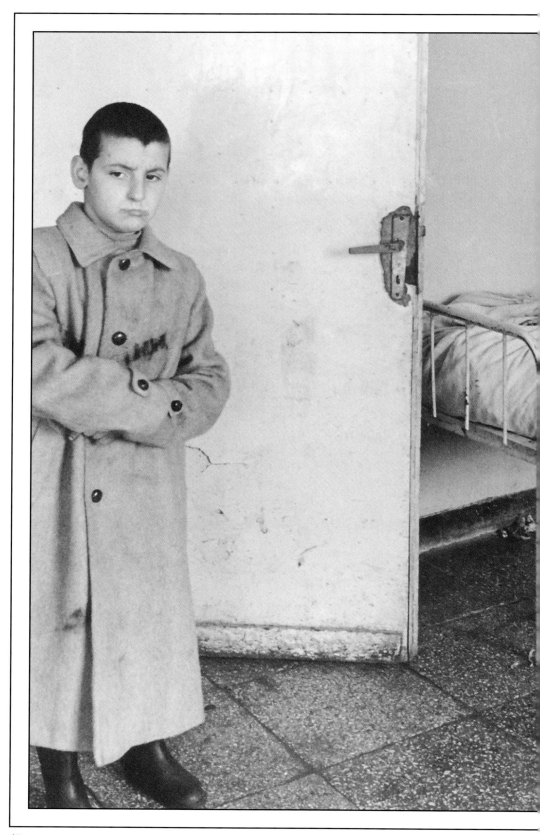

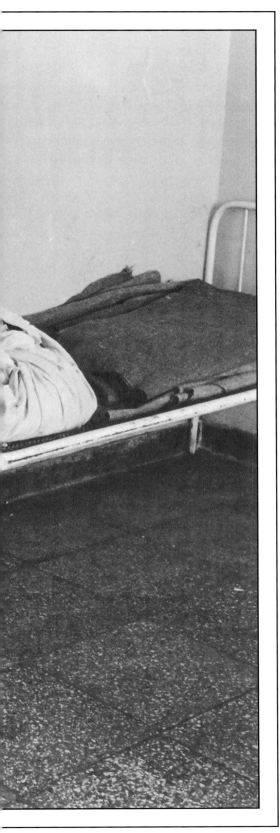

outside the orphanage had grown, people were climbing over the walls and surrounding the vehicles.

Already, a couple of bags had been stolen off a roof rack.

38. A hurried consultation with the Albanian Democrats sadly concluded that our presence was drawing attention to the building, making it a potential target for robbers once we had left. Many of the crowd outside, we were told, believed that we should be looking after them and their children, not wasting aid on children that no one cared for.

Life is valued very differently in that desperately poor country.

39. Reluctantly, the decision was taken that there was little more that we could accomplish in Albania, in fact, our being there would be more of a hindrance than a help.

The Albanian Democrats were caught in a dilemma – they did not want us to leave, but recognised that our presence made the orderly distribution of the aid much more difficult.

40. With the assurances that the aid would be distributed as agreed and that they would ensure that it would stay with the people for whom it was intended, we headed north for the Yugoslavian border at Hani Hotit.

41. At the border the support vehicles separated, three heading for Budapest, two for Dubrovnik and two for Romania."

IN SUMMARY:

"We had taken twenty trucks and seven support vehicles with over seven hundred tonnes of aid to Albania – the largest convoy since World War Two.

All the aid arrived safely in Albania and all the people and vehicles returned safely.

We followed the advice of The Red Cross, unloaded into guarded compounds and used local transport for distribution.

We saw the aid delivered to the orphanages and evidence to help us believe that it would stay where it was intended.

We used the most organised party in Albania – the Albanian Democrats to make the local arrangements. They knew they had to succeed if they were to get more of the same help they so desperately needed".

Concluding thoughts:
"Quite a remarkable achievement".

John Dawson
March 1992.

Tom couldn't wait to reach his little brother and sister – did he have a surprise for them.

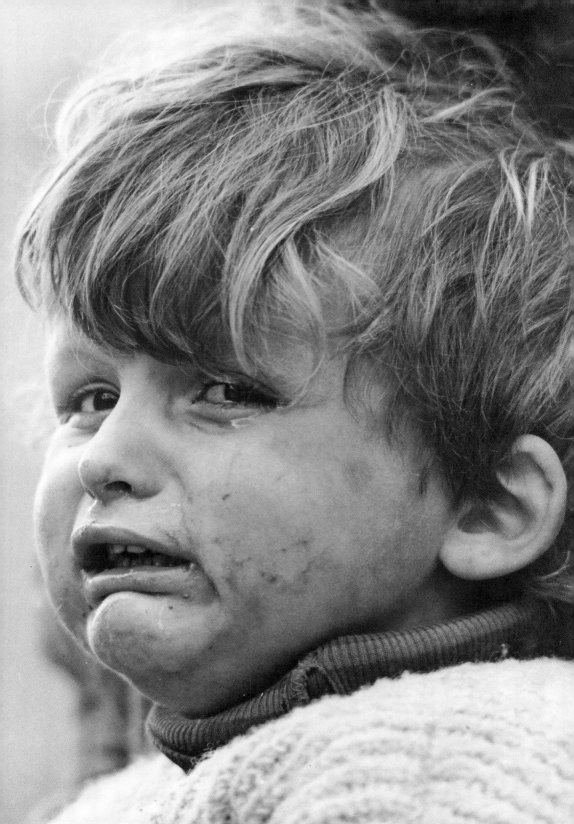

It would take more than a warm sweater to comfort this lonely boy in February 1992.

FOOTPRINTS

ONE night a man dreamed he was walking along a beach with the Lord. Across the sky flashed scenes from his life in which there were two sets of footprints in the sand; one belonging to him, and the other to the Lord. But he saw that at the saddest points of his life, there was only one set of footprints. "Lord! You said that once I decided to follow you, you'd never leave me. So why, during my most troublesome times, is there only one set of footprints?" The Lord replied, "My son, my precious child, I love you and would never leave you. During your times of trial and suffering, when you see only one set of footprints, it was then that I carried you."

4
THE BIBLE

As John Dawson had remarked "our untimely exodus from the compound in Shkodra really was a very frightening experience." I remember it well.

The whole compound was surrounded by thousands of people all desperate for food and clothing. A battalion of soldiers guarded the compound from within but they too, deprived of even the most basic essentials, began to steal from the trucks, and this only incited the crowd more.

From our point of view, we had a major problem. The men who were supposed to be the ones to protect us and the aid, were the ones who were stealing it from us. Virtually every soldier had a Kalashnikov automatic rifle in one hand and a box of food or a bundle of clothing in the other. On several occasions we tried to take the aid away from them *but they would respond by pointing their guns at us*. The team's safety was of paramount importance to me and the thought of someone getting killed for the sake of a black bin liner full of clothing wasn't worth thinking about.

I remember vividly two old ladies at the gate begging for food, pleading with their outstretched hands and a soldier smashing them with the butt of his rifle. I couldn't take it any longer and went to stop him. As I did so he caught sight of me and spun round, his rifle cocked, index finger on the trigger, and if I hadn't stopped in my tracks I am convinced he would have shot me.

"OK" I said backing up. I could see he was no more than seventeen years old and was as scared as I was. Thankfully he left the old ladies alone.

The trucks were all unloaded by this time and I quickly gathered the nine drivers together. They were all going out through the border crossing at Hani Hotit, some twenty miles to the north and I asked them all to keep their tilt sheets rolled up, so the townspeople could see they were empty and not worth attacking.

I asked the police chief to have forty policemen at the main gate at precisely 2.00 p.m. when all nine trucks would leave in convoy. The drivers were told to "go for your life, stay in tight formation and not to stop for anyone".

Fortunately it worked and the townspeople were kept back out of the compound. I decided to take the initiative and get the support team out

Two old ladies pleading for food at a Shkodra compound in February 1992. The soldiers responded by smashing their outstretched hands with the butts of their rifles.

with our seven vehicles before being overwhelmed and having the vehicles stripped. The thought of leaving someone behind was too frightening to contemplate, so after a quick head-count, my white Opel hire car and the six four-wheel drive vehicles sped out of that tinder box and didn't stop until they had reached the border at Hani Hotit and passed safely into Montenegro.

As we stepped onto Yugoslavian soil, the thirty man support team, all safe and sound, breathed a very big sigh of relief. Close to the customs point was a large parking area which we utilized to have lunch, before separating as we had agreed, each making their own way back to England.

After my accident with the Range Rover, I had hired a white Opel automatic car from Avis in Budapest. I always felt extremely guilty for not telling them I was going 'touring' in Albania with their rent-a-car, and here I had only three days left to get it back to Budapest.

All my life I had wanted to visit the old walled city of Dubrovnik and now it was so close. Although the city had been damaged in the war with Serbia, we were led to believe the fighting had finished and without doubt this was an opportunity too good to miss.

A burned out petrol station on the road to Dubrovnic

When I informed the others of my intention to go off alone, Azad Kumar said he would like to come with me. Arthur Tooms, the well known Stamford antique restorer, who like Azad Kumar, had been a pillar of strength on that trip, said he would like to come too, along with four others.

So saying goodbye to the rest of the team, Azad Kumar came in the Opel with me, whilst Arthur drove the Land Rover Defender. Vic Kaye from Ampthill in Bedfordshire was given the seat of honour in the Defender and the remaining seats were occupied by Stuart Bennett, Stephen Clay and Kevin Burton.

Driving through the beautiful scenery of Montenegro, we headed for Titograd and then on to the coastal town of Lepetane. There we caught the ferry and went island hopping down the Croatian coast towards Dubrovnik.

I'm jumping the gun a little, for on our arrival at Lepetane we were informed that we had missed the last ferry so decided to stay the night there and sought out a dockside cafe for some refreshment. The cafe was full of blue uniformed militia and we were approached by an English speaking officer by the name of Vladimir. When he discovered we wished to visit Dubrovnik, he informed us there was no problem whatsoever.

We were now only about one mile from the walled city and I felt sure as we rounded the next bend it would be in view.

A line of twenty or so soldiers from the Yugoslavian National Army, automatic rifles pointed at us, straddled the road. I eased back on the throttle and brought the Opel to a halt, a few feet from their commanding officer. The Defender drew up behind me.

"You're English?" he asked, "Yes," I replied. "What are you doing here?" he demanded. "We're going to Dubrovnik," I answered, showing him our pass. "We understood the ceasefire came into operation at 7.00 a.m. this morning." "Well, that's true," said the officer. "However, I have some bad news for you. The ceasefire was broken at 9.30 a.m. – it lasted for just two and a half hours. Turn around and go back about five miles and on your left you will see a road that will take you to Trebinje. Where are you heading for eventually?" I told him Belgrade and then on into Hungary, so he suggested from Trebinje we should make for Sarajevo, Zvornic and Novi Sad.

At that precise moment there was an almighty explosion just over the hill not more than two hundred yards away. The ground beneath us vibrated violently as if an earthquake was happening and our vehicles were physically moving up and down. The noise was deafening.

He hadn't been kidding – the ceasefire had been broken. We had to get out of there, quickly, and the officer very kindly sent one of his men with us to Trebinje, to show us the way.

It turned out this soldier was a black belt 2nd level in judo and when he discovered we all practised karate, there was an immediate bond between us. As we parted, heading westwards into the Bosnian mountains, I gave him a copy of my *Beginners Guide to Shotokan Karate* as a small token for his trouble. In that moment amidst the madness of war, a bond was forged between martial artists which seemed to give him renewed hope. As we drove away, watching him waving till we were out of sight, produced a feeling of unusual sadness. We all knew deep down that our paths would not cross again.

The rest of the daylight hours were spent climbing high into the mountains of Bosnia Herzegovina and as dusk fell we slipped quietly through Sarajevo. The city was calm, with the bulk of the fighting and devastation still to come. Groups of soldiers 'hung around' on street corners. We had the feeling of a 'lull before the storm.'

It had been snowing heavily and fortunately for us, the snowploughs had been out. We were now on the mountain road to Zvornic and were climbing higher and higher. Snow was piled six feet high on either side of the road and the pine forests were laden with snow to breaking point.

We had been driving for about three hours and it was snowing hard. The snowflakes were so big and plentiful, the windscreen wipers were labouring under the strain. The road on which we were travelling was quite a lonely one and there had been no towns or villages for the past thirty miles.

The weather had worsened and we appeared to be in the middle of a snowstorm, visibility was down to five yards and if there were any road signs they had become completely camouflaged.

There was no doubt, all of us were becoming very anxious indeed and with the temperature outside minus twenty degrees celsius, spending a night in the car was not an enthralling notion. Realistically, the chances of finding an hotel open at night, in the middle of winter, in the middle of a war, were pretty slim.

We drove on through the night when suddenly I saw what just might be a signpost. Pulling up, I walked back to it and brushed the snow away. The sign was rectangular and in black letters on a white background I read the word 'Socolac.' The others came over and joined me, "Eureka, civilization" shouted Arthur Tooms, the oldest and most stable member of the group. Then it was back to the motors, a left turn off the highway and soon we were driving along the high street of the most picturesque village we had ever seen. The whole village was covered in snow and the cars that lined both sides of the road obviously hadn't moved for a very long time.

The village's only hotel lay on our right and I went in alone to enquire if it was open and had any vacancies. As I approached the reception desk, I noticed a number of children playing games on the steps. They were enjoying each other's company and took little notice of me.

The hotel manager appeared and after shaking hands, accompanied me to the first floor. There were seven of us, so we really needed four double rooms. As he spoke to me, going up the stairs, I realised he had quite a good command of the English language. I also noticed his breath vaporizing as it left his mouth.

There was no heating whatsoever in the hotel, nor had there been any for many months. The bedrooms were beyond belief. They were wet, dank and musty, the walls were covered with mould and some very interesting mosaics of fungi had materialised in the corners. The bed sheets felt as if they had been 'spun dry' in a washing machine and then put straight on the bed – 'damp' wasn't the word. My inspection of the rooms was merely a formality, simply a ritual. The choice was simple, we either slept in the car or settled for the only 'available accommodation' in town.

Mounted on the wall in the hotel reception was a complex of pigeon holes, a large honeycombed affair that had obviously seen better days. Now the little boxes were all empty except for seven passports in just four of them.

Although we were very tired, the thought of slipping between the sheets was not terribly appealing, so I suggested a compromise of laying our waterproof sleeping bags on top of the beds and sleeping in them. This met with unanimous approval. Certainly, we could avoid the rapid onset of pneumonia.

None of us had eaten all day and we were absolutely famished. Somewhat apprehensively we made our way to the dining room on the ground floor. It was spacious, drab and empty. Choosing a table for seven was not difficult from the seventy or so on offer. All were bare, none set, as no guests were expected.

A door from the kitchen opened and a waiter came in. He bore a strange resemblance to the hotel manager whom I had seen earlier. He spoke English, "Good evening," he said, "We have soup and bread." Kevin Burton, one of three young lads from Royston in Hertfordshire and all on their first trip (and their last!) asked what else he had. "Nothing, of course" came the answer. We all looked at each other. "Sounds good to me," echoed around the table, and with that, 'Basil' (from the T.V. series Fawlty Towers) as he later became known, disappeared.

It was freezing in the room but still condensation poured down the windows. Two young girls looking terribly sombre appeared and set the table, after which, the kitchen door swung open and a rather large lady waddled in carrying an enormous steaming urn. She ladled the hot broth into our bowls and as the steam rose, you could hardly make out who was sitting opposite you at the table. 'Basil' and the girls arrived with full plates of freshly baked bread. We were ravenous.

All conversation ceased abruptly as we dunked large chunks of bread into the hot broth. It was indeed 'manna from heaven'. The two girls stood in silence – mesmerized. The large lady returned carrying a huge carafe of red wine, which in reality, was the cheapest and most unappealing wine I've ever had but given the circumstances it was fabulous.

We sat back and asked 'Basil' to come and join us. Steven Clay fetched him a glass and half filled it. "Thank you very much indeed Basil – that was wonderful," I said, "but may I ask you a question – something has been puzzling me!"

I wanted to know where all those children came from that we had seen earlier playing near the reception. He pulled himself up in his seat as if to compose himself, his smile disappeared and he sighed audibly. The youngest of the two girls, who was about eleven years old, began to cry. I felt terrible. I wished I hadn't asked the question. 'Basil' opened his mouth and began to speak.

The hotel at Socolac – temporary respite for 200 children from the injustices of war.

"There are two hundred children staying at this hotel. All of them are orphans who have lost their mothers and fathers in the last week and have been brought here from the fighting in Croatia." It went very quiet indeed – no-one else spoke.

"They stay here for just a few days and then are shipped out to foster parents all over the country." He looked at the two girls who had been serving at the table. "They don't know it yet but they will be leaving tomorrow." "Where to?" I asked. He just shook his head.

The next morning we awoke to the sound of children singing. It was a beautiful day but very cold. We made our way through the reception area and out to the vehicles. We had all decided the night before that whatever rations and sweets we had on board we would share out amongst the children.

They were so thankful and excited. It was such a joy to see the smiles on their little faces.

I don't know at what precise moment a thought occurred to me, or why, I just know it did!

Some twenty days previously the convoy had left Kempston Police Headquarters in Bedford. Thousands of people were there to see it off and the media were there in strength. The Lord Lieutenant of Bedfordshire, Mr. Samuel Whitbread, made a speech followed by other dignitaries, until finally, the Reverend Carter blessed the convoy.

Towards the end of his speech, he called me out and handed me a large coloured pictorial Bible – a children's Bible and said, "John, I want you to take this Bible and give it to the orphaned children of Albania. It will give them hope from the people of Bedfordshire."

With that, he handed me the book and I returned to my place and later packed it safely away. In all the turmoil and confusion in Albania, I completely forgot about the present and so failed to do what I had promised.

The Lord Lieutenant of Bedfordshire, Mr. Samuel Whitbread, cutting the ribbon to mark the beginning of the convoy's momentous journey.

Rushing outside through the snow to my car, I grabbed my green kit-bag and thrust my arm down to the bottom. I felt something hard! Yes – it was still there.

Bringing it back into the hotel reception I asked the manager, who looked remarkably like 'Basil' the waiter, (well he would! – they were the same person but dressed accordingly) if he would help.

In the centre of the reception was a

The Reverend Carter from Kempston prepares to hand over The Children's Bible – a present to Albanian orphaned children from the people of Bedford.

circular table with seven children's chairs, so we arranged the first seven children around the table. They were told they had fifteen minutes to read and look at the book, then it would be the turn of the next seven. They all had a smattering of English and understood from the beautifully coloured pictures the stories of the parables.

I stood back in amazement. They knew Jesus. They recognised him immediately. Pointing and chattering and laughing and teaching each other, it was a wonderful moment for them and for us. For I knew in that split second we had transformed that hotel – that orphanage – into a one book library and I marvelled at the irony of it all.

That Bible, given in good faith for orphaned Albanian children was actually meant for orphaned Croatian children, hundreds of miles away in another time and another place.

The fact was that when that book was given by the Reverend Carter, all those Croatian children were still living happily at home with their parents.

A further irony perhaps! – *Perhaps not!!*

Total despondency as team members arrive in Budapest after their emotional 'Socolac experience'.

...diers standing guard over TFA's aid consignment at the Shkodra ...mpound.

...shback to 1992 — mentally handicapped children at the Shkodra institute ...nforted by warm clothing and blankets brought from England.

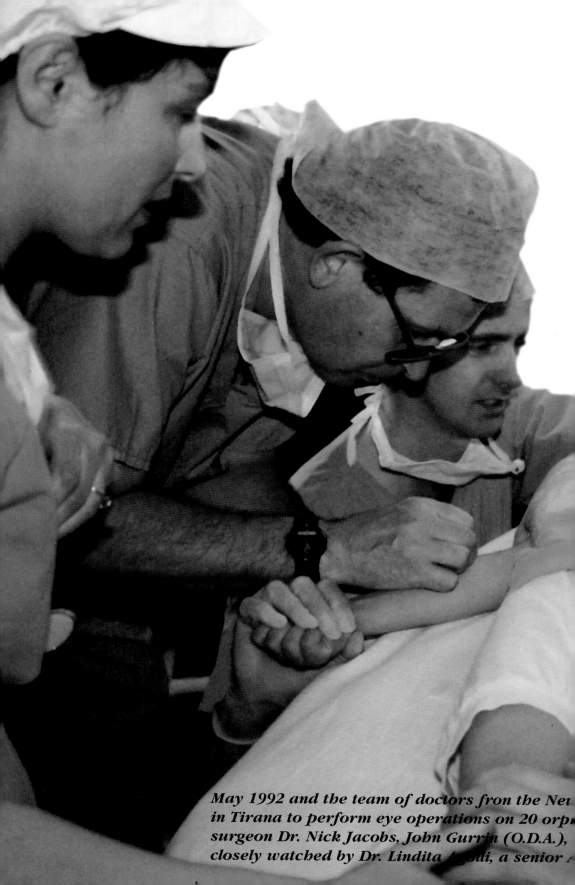

May 1992 and the team of doctors from the New
in Tirana to perform eye operations on 20 orp
surgeon Dr. Nick Jacobs, John Gurrin (O.D.A.),
closely watched by Dr. Lindita A....li, a senior

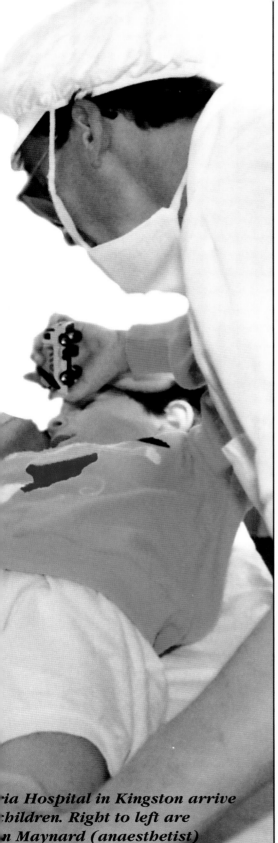

...ria Hospital in Kingston arrive
...hildren. Right to left are
...n Maynard (anaesthetist)
...n anaesthetist.

5 THE BRITISH DOCTORS

I n his capacity as a BBC News Correspondent together with cameraman Bhasker Solanki, Bill Hamilton accompanied Task Force Albania and a surgical team from the New Victoria Hospital in Kingston-upon-Thames on a dramatic rescue mission. It was matron Mirjam Noonja at Shkodra's Teufik G'yli orphanage who first alerted me to the plight of certain blind children and thanks to the concern and generosity of Charles Hutton, Chief Executive at the 'New Vic.,' along with Nick Jacobs, John Maynard and John Gurrin, the ophthalmological team, the outcome was, in Bill's words, what "no-one dared predict." Bill takes up the story –

In a country where tens of thousands of people are engaged in a daily battle for survival, news of the presence of a Good Samaritan travels like wildfire. As the clamour for aid grows louder by the day, so too does the intolerable pressure on those whose mission is to provide whatever relief they can. So when John van Weenen returned to Shkodra to satisfy himself that his Task Force deliveries had reached their intended targets, he found himself confronted time and again with further pleas for help.

There had been evidence of theft in some institutions, a distinctly noticeable improvement in others, with clear signs that the children were not only delighted with the clothes that had reached them but, more importantly, had gained a degree of self confidence that had been so visibly lacking on earlier visits. Nowhere was this more evident than inside the city's largest orphanage where the new owners of Dennis the Menace and Desperate Dan T-shirts were behaving in a manner not dissimilar to the antics of the cartoon characters emblazoned across their chests. Those were the sights and the moments that make all the sacrifices so worthwhile.

As for the Lincolnshire man who dispatched fifty litre tins of paint . . . if only he could have seen the relish of the caretaker as he mounted a makeshift ladder to give the place its first internal decoration in more than twenty years!

Alas, not all were joining in the fun. In the dormitory next door nurses were worried about the condition of other recent arrivals. The matron, unable to hold back the tears a minute longer, rushed into the room clutching four of the youngest children. "You've got to do something for these poor creatures . . . The doctor says they'll all be blind within weeks, and there's nothing he can recommend and nowhere he can take them. I beg you . . . take them back to London . . . if they have nothing else, they're surely entitled to their sight."

Van Weenen felt a shiver pass down his spine. He looked at the children by now in obvious distress. One little lad, Klodian, just five years old, was already blind in one eye. A scribbled note in his file indicated he had just thirty per cent vision in the other. Two of the other cases were similarly distressing.

By now matron Mirjam Nooja was inconsolable. What had started barely an hour before as a happy reunion was degenerating into an uncomfortable and painful experience. As van Weenen made for the front door, promising to make whatever sensible enquiries he could, the matron chased after him, the children still in tow. "Take them now," she pleaded again. "You've got doctors over there who can do the job . . . please, please . . ."

Van Weenen did what he could to calm the situation. Even if it was possible to get tickets and visas for these children to come to Britain, he insisted, "then the trauma of leaving the only place they have ever known, never mind having to sit in a car and an aircraft would be just overwhelming. "I'll go back and see what can be done, but this time I'm afraid I cannot hold out any promises."

With that he bade farewell and left, barely able to summon up enough courage to turn his head to offer a parting wave from the end of the dusty pot-holed drive along which few ever bothered to venture.

Arriving home in Northamptonshire van Weenen slept uneasily for nights. He simply had to find a solution to the problem. After all that had been achieved he could not bear the thought of those children – so young and so desperately unfortunate – losing their sight. He told his wife: "If I have to walk the length and breadth of Harley Street for a whole week, I'll find the right people. The orphans cannot come here, so we'll have to persuade surgeons to go there. There's no other answer."

Easier said than done. Where was van Weenen going to find an ophthalmic surgical team willing to extricate themselves even for a few days from their burdensome diary of clinics and surgery at a time when waiting lists were stretching for many months ahead?

As he wrestled with the problem, a thought suddenly crossed his mind. He hurried upstairs to his office and excitedly began to finger his way through the index file listing the names of all those who had contributed goods to his Task Force convoy.

The search went on for hours. Then at last, a stroke of luck. Under the letter M appeared the name of Dr. John Maynard. Van Weenen had a vivid recollection of the day Dr. Maynard had driven to Bedford from his London home with sacks of clothes collected by his family and a box of assorted medical equipment he had obtained from a number of hospitals where he worked as an anaesthetist. He had even left his telephone number.

The call was immediate. Would Dr. Maynard be interested in making a mercy dash to Albania? And, more importantly, did he know of any eye surgeons who would be willing to accompany him? Not surprisingly, Dr. Maynard wanted more precise information. What would be required? What equipment did the Albanians have? Did anyone keep proper medical records of the orphans' condition? How long was it anticipated that the mission would last? The questions were endless, and there were few answers. Van Weenen had neither the knowledge not the medical expertise to put Dr. Maynard properly in the picture.

"What I do know, Dr. Maynard, is that some of these children are losing their sight and there is neither the will nor know-how in Albania to prevent it happening. You are my only hope."

As he put the phone down, Dr. Maynard felt that a heavy burden of responsibility had suddenly been thrust upon his shoulders. He looked across at his wife Gill and their four children, Jennie seventeen, Jo her thirteen year old sister, Tom eight, and the baby of the family, Lucy just two. There they were . . . four lovely children – fit, healthy and intelligent. They had everything they wanted in life and more besides. Yet here was another dreadful picture. Orphans deprived even of a few hours in the fresh air, never mind all the things that children in England take for granted and now they were going blind. If it would be difficult to say 'Yes' then it would be much more difficult to say 'No'. Putting my hand in my pocket would have been relatively simple, but not the same as getting off my backside and doing something. I knew I had to go and I believed I knew the very man to join me.'

The man he had in mind was one of Britain's most eminent ophthalmic surgeons. Across Surrey and South London, Dr. Nick Jacobs was in great demand for his operating skills. National Health and private patients alike spoke highly of his work. Here was a man who embodied all the positive traits of the English surgeon – great dignity, warmth and a powerful inner strength and integrity.

Dr. Jacobs too had a young family. The two arranged a meeting with van Weenen and the Chief Executive of the New Victoria Hospital at Kingston-upon-Thames, Charles Hutton. Though all remained apprehensive about what might be involved, it was decided – whatever the risks and uncertainty - that the team should leave at the earliest possible opportunity.

Van Weenen had done it again. He could hardly have hand picked a better team. The New Victoria Hospital is recognized as an intimate, independent hospital whose friendly, caring atmosphere and high level of medical skills have earned it a fine reputation well beyond the bounds of Kingston.

There was an additional bonus. The hospital had retained its charitable status and any surplus made from treating private patients is either re-invested or donated to charity in the form of free medical treatment. It was decided on this occasion that such charity should be extended to the Albanian children and that the hospital would pay the entire cost of the mission, though the team would give their services voluntarily.

Within days Dr. Jacobs, Dr. Maynard and operating assistant John Gurrin were airborne, flying, they said, into the unknown and carrying everything they could think of. Despite numerous attempts to get detailed information about the state of the operating theatre at Tirana's No. 1 Hospital, they had very little to go on. As they settled into their Swissair seats for a breathtaking view of the rugged alpine summits glistening in the glorious summer sunshine, there were unspoken fears that the whole venture might prove an unmitigated disaster.

The Albanian Government extended its usual courtesy at the airport. Dr. Tritan Shehu, the tall, handsome and engaging Minister of Health, was waiting at the foot of the aircraft steps after it had taxied to a standstill. He had even laid on official transport to take the surgical team straight to their hotel.

A few hours later the doctors found themselves ushered into Shehu's office situated on the top floor of the Health Ministry building just a few hundred yards from Tirana's main boulevard, Sheritorja 'Deshmoret e Kombit' (Avenue of the Martyrs of the Nation).

The Minister's large, simply furnished room was in a chaotic state. At least three meetings were proceeding at the same time. Shehu was scrambling from one group to the other, trying to keep abreast of what was happening in order to bring some sensible conclusion to each discussion. In another corner of the room anxious Parliamentary deputies were pressing for his attention, while a Ministry official was trying to explain the workings of a portable telephone, something of an innovation in this part of the Balkans.

By this time I had managed to squeeze my way through the door too, hoping to secure an interview the Minister had promised the BBC. In a scene more reminiscent of a Saturday street market, something or someone had to give.

The civil servants hurriedly concluded their business, rose from their seats, offered a polite nod and left in silence, demonstrating an intuitive understanding of a guest's needs. Somehow I could not imagine such happenings in the corridors of Whitehall!

Shehu offered his apologies for keeping us waiting. I was soon to discover why foreigners were given pride of place. The Minister was in a dreadful state, papers piled high on his desk, lists of important contacts with whom he must get in touch, a fax machine which had broken down yet again. The sweat was pouring from his brow.

Lili Boshnjaku, matron at the home for mentally handicapped children standing on the left with 14 year old Anila who had been blind from birth. Also in the picture are the visually impaired children, the director and nurses of the 'Teufik G'yli' orphanage in Shkodra.

"Shall we do the interview now?" he asked hesitantly.

I suggested he wiped his forehead and put on a tie. It would look more authoritative that way.

Of course, he was pleased to see the ophthalmic team from London. "You have no idea just how much this means to us . . . how much encouragement it gives. You won't believe it, Bill, when I tell you this country's health budget for the coming year. It's zero . . . I have not been given a penny to spend. That's the legacy of forty-five years of communist rule. We need everything . . . medicines, syringes, blood bags. We are so dependent on western aid and we have a massive reorganization of the health service to put in hand. Anything you can do will be appreciated."

Listening just a few feet away, Dr. Maynard and Dr. Jacobs winced. What on earth could they expect to find in the operating theatre? If conditions were really as bad as this, would they be in a position to carry out the sight-saving surgery?

Dr. Maynard asked to be taken to the hospital at once. Van Weenen, cameraman Bhas Solanki and myself were left to make arrangements to ensure the Shkodra orphans would be collected by minibus the following morning for the two and a half hour journey to Tirana. It was vital everything should go according to plan so as to minimize any anxiety or stress on the part of the children, few of whom had ever left the orphanage grounds before.

We left Shkodra at dawn, reducing the risk of running into an ambush. The road to the north is a favourite hunting ground for the brigands eager to profit in a country threatened by an unacceptable level of lawlessness. The police can do little, in part because they lack crime-fighting tools such as fast cars and computers. In addition, many of them are despised as being too closely identified with the repressive regime of the past. Fearing reprisals from organized criminals, they rarely intervene to maintain order.

The crimes had been increasing in brazenness as well as number. Just a few days before, a group of Albanians had ambushed a foreigner whose car had crashed into a ditch. They stole everything they could carry, including technical equipment, food, tapes and clothing. They even dismantled and stole parts of the car itself. When the police eventually arrived, they appeared totally unable to control the mob and left without assisting the helpless driver.

Even the Minister of Justice was reported to have fallen victim to the crime wave, robbed by bandits at a roadblock.

In the event, our journey passed without incident and arriving ahead of schedule, we decided to pay another visit to the institute for mentally handicapped children. The matron, Lili Boshnjaku, was delighted to see us, but save for a remarkable improvement in the condition of little

Albert, the rate of progress was still depressingly slow.

As our eyes scanned the familiar faces spread out across the dank, stone floor, in an instant we found ourselves drawn to a half-naked, pathetic figure slumped against the barred window overlooking the filthy weed-ridden courtyard.

A more miserable existence it is difficult to imagine. Abandoned by her parents, Anila, thought to be fourteen years old, had lost her sight years ago while locked away in this miserable place. She had developed two cataracts – one in each eye – and had become totally blind. What's more it was thought that what few tranquillizers were ever on offer here might have been responsible for Anila's condition.

In that instant, we took a decision. Anila would return to Tirana with us. What Dr. Jacobs would say we could not be sure, but we believed he would want to do everything he could to try to restore Anila's sight. We told the matron to have Anila ready to move within the hour.

Half a mile away at the Teufik G'yli orphanage, Klodian and five other children had been tidily dressed and were eagerly awaiting the arrival of the minibus.

Hours went by, but still it did not come. Frantic attempts were made to reach Tirana by phone. It was impossible to get through.

As darkness approached we started south, promising the bus would arrive next morning come what may. There was simply no way in which we could have accommodated all the children in our already crammed vehicle and the orphanage insisted they must all travel as a group. The sense of disappointment was overwhelming. Six hours of surgery had already been lost and Dr. Jacobs and his team were only in Albania for four days.

Health Ministry officials apologized profusely, explained that the minibus driver had refused to travel to Shkodra on the grounds that it was much too dangerous and promised faithfully that a replacement driver would leave at first light next day. Shehu was so angry and embarrassed over the incident that he ordered the driver to telephone him personally at the precise moment of departure.

He duly obliged. The only difficulty this time was getting the children to board the bus. Two were terrified, kicking and screaming, unable to be consoled. They had never ventured out of the front door of the orphanage in all of their six years.

By now Dr. Jacobs and Dr. Maynard had been able to examine the theatre in which they would have to carry out their operations. "It was like something straight out of Charles Dickens; incredible squalor, a lack of any kind of organization and a dearth of equipment. We were shocked."

There was, however, one completely unexpected asset. The ophthalmic microscope, once airlifted from Germany for the exclusive use of the country's former dictator, Enver Hoxha, had been seized from the family home. Now, for the first time, hundreds of ordinary Albanian children could enjoy the benefits of micro surgery.

Yet for years Hoxha had boasted of his achievements in building a Health Service that he insisted was the envy of most of the world. "What we have done is evidence of the socialist humanism, which characterizes the people's power, of the reality of Albania where man is considered the most precious character."

To be fair, Hoxha's regime could claim, with some justification, that it had done a good deal to improve health and social welfare. Expenditure, he once said, for the maintenance of all the health institutions at the time of King Zog was less than the entire pay roll of the King's courtiers. That problem was addressed by providing free medical treatment, and building more hospitals and clinics. Doctor-patient ratios were improved and the average life expectancy rose from fifty-three in 1950 to sixty-eight in 1982. Yet compared with its Eastern European neighbours, the health service was riddled with shortcomings and inadequacies, not least the interminable waiting for sub-standard medical equipment arriving by ship from China.

A likely pair of ophthalmologists. The author with Bill Hamilton.

Certainly Hoxha's repeated claims that only Marxist-Leninist ideals create the conditions needed to transform people's health was a blatant contradiction of almost everything Albanian doctors and nurses were having to face every day of the week. Though to have expressed such sentiments would have cost them not just their jobs but, very probably, a lengthy term in gaol.

Today it's a very different story. The medical staff are only too willing to let everyone know of their frustrations. Most operating theatres lack even the most elementary equipment such as surgical gloves, disinfectant, scalpels and catgut used as a thread to stitch the wounds.

Drs. Jacobs, Maynard and Gurrin had come prepared for the worst and by now were desperate to get on with their work. They decided first to perform a series of half-hour operations correcting many of the squints which, alas, are all too prevalent among so many of Albania's underprivileged children. All went well.

So tight was their schedule that for most of the time two operations were going on in the same theatre. Sulejman Zhugli, Albania's leading eye surgeon, was in charge of the second operating table. Dr. Jacobs was astounded by the quality of his work, given the primitive conditions in which he was forced to operate. Giving of his time here without any thought of remuneration seemed a very small sacrifice to Dr. Jacobs when he enquired what his Albanian colleague was earning. "The equivalent of twenty-five US dollars a month," came the reply, "but at least I have the satisfaction of doing some good."

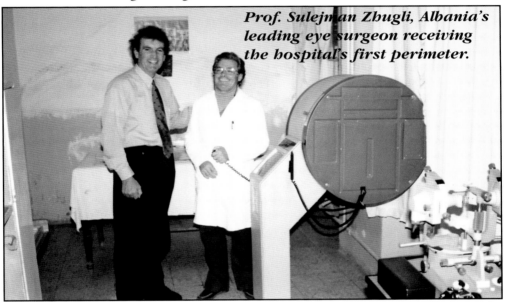

Prof. Sulejman Zhugli, Albania's leading eye surgeon receiving the hospital's first perimeter.

Just how much good was soon evident. Hearing of the English team's visit, adults and children alike were surging down the hospital corridors, hammering on the doors of the operating theatre and clamouring to be seen. So disturbing was the noise and so great the fear of invasion, Dr. Jacobs had to give an assurance he would hold an emergency clinic between operations. The pressures were building on all sides.

In a tiny ante-room a nurse had emptied some coffee into a small cooking pot and was holding it in a near vertical position over the rusted elements of an electric fire. it would be quite some time before even a lukewarm drink would be available. Not that heat was any sort of a problem in this instance. Everyone who had the merest connection with Hospital No. 1 it seemed, was crowded into the theatre, marvelling at Dr. Jacob's work and eager to learn and profit from the experience.

Now it was little Emiliano's turn. He had already lost all vision in one eye and glaucoma had reduced vision in the other to a little over four per cent. Total blindness was only a matter of months away. Glaucoma, the surgeon explained, is a defect that takes place in front of the coloured iris. The eye fluid does not drain away quickly enough causing an increase in pressure, damaging the nerve and making the eye grow too large.

If the children were secretly nervous there were no outward signs as they sat holding hands with the orphanage staff and quietly waiting their turn. Toys had even been brought from Britain to help pass the time.

It was another piece of baggage, however, that was to be at the centre of a theatre crisis, and which would be paramount not just in saving sight but life itself. Dr. Maynard had been particularly worried about the anaesthetics available, so he brought his own, together with a saturation monitor, a lightweight piece of technology which gives a visual indication of the amount of oxygen in the blood stream. Dr. Lindita Agolli, attractive, intelligent and one of Albania's most respected anaesthetists, was surprised at such sophistication. A fluent English speaker, she was particularly keen to play an active role in Dr. Maynard's work. Indeed, she was first to spot something going horribly wrong.

Klodian was on the table. He had entered the theatre ever so calmly and within minutes a highly complicated operation was under way. Suddenly, the sound of an alarm could be heard and, as Dr. Agolli and Dr. Maynard glanced down at the monitor, they knew urgent and decisive action was required. The oxygen levels had dropped very suddenly and very rapidly.

Klodian's blood pressure was increased using a drug that stimulates the heart, ephidrine being injected intravenously. Without the little machine, Klodian might well have died in the operating theatre. "We could have had a disaster on our hands," Dr. Maynard told his Albanian colleague, "so I am going to leave you this monitor. You don't know how many lives it may save."

A few minutes' break was called for, but Dr. Jacobs was determined to honour all his pledges. The hospital director, overwhelmed by the numbers jostling on the stairs in their desperation to reach the English surgeon, set aside the biggest room in the building for an afternoon clinic.

For a time, pandemonium ensued. A policeman, presumably called to try and keep some semblance of order seemed more interested in obtaining a premier position in the queue. It almost looked as if everyone in Tirana had some kind of eye problem. Even though most appreciated there was simply no way in which Dr. Jacobs could treat their ailment, just 'being seen' seemed to bring some sense of relief.

Back in the theatre, and preparations for the arrival of Anila. She had been brought from the institute for mentally handicapped children in

Shkodra still wearing her ill-fitting rags. No one had bothered to give her a shower, not even a cursory wash. This was symbolic of the way the country had regarded such children over so many years. Here at last, one of them was about to get some special attention, first in the list of someone's priorities.

Anila was to provide the hardest test of the surgeon's skills. Dr. Jacobs had examined her thoroughly. Though her deteriorating cataract condition had now left her totally blind, there was an outside chance of restoring some degree of vision to one of her eyes.

Within the hour, the news came that everyone wanted to hear. Anila might just be able to see again. Dr. Jacobs, encouraged that the damage behind one of the pupils could be partially repaired, delicately set to work again, Hoxha's microscope proving a more than satisfactory aid to the painstakingly detailed work.

After two hours of intricate surgery the operation was over and Anila was wheeled back into the ward. It would not be long before the surgical team would discover if their endeavours would bring the result for which everyone had been earnestly hoping and praying.

Next day the bandages came off. From all directions children, doctors, nurses, cleaners hustled for a place by the bedside. The suspense, for all, quite unbearable.

Anila sat up quietly and pursed her lips to a tight wistful smile. She pulled a banana from the hand of a highly emotional Lili Boshnjaku, moved it close to her chin and began to split open the skin.

"Une shoh!" she whispered, "I can see."

At that loud cheers rang out across the ward. It was hard to ascertain who was more excited. Dr. Jacobs emptied half a dozen 'Smarties' into Anila's left hand. She bent forwards for a few moments, clearly trying to focus on the luminous multi-coloured chocolate beans.

"Go on, then, count them!" Dr. Jacobs urged.

"Nje, dy, tre, kater, pese . . . " Anila counted, pointing to each sweet in turn.

It was the outcome no one – least of all Dr. Jacobs and Dr. Maynard – had dared to predict. It also convinced them whatever the difficulties, they must return. They did. Within weeks.

Conclusion of the excerpt from Albania Who Cares?

The author takes up the story:

In the meantime, Task Force Albania, in conjunction with the New Victoria Hospital, organized visits to London for Professor Sulejman Zhugli, head of Tirana's ophthalmological unit, anaesthetist Dr. Lindita Agolli and paediatrician Dr. Linda Ciu. All three visited the UK's top teaching hospitals and on their return to Albania, instigated seminars in

*Dr. Lindita Agolli,
one of Albania's finest
anaesthetists.*

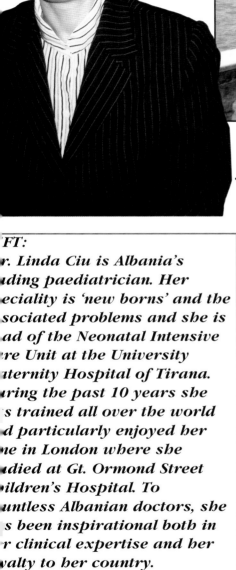

*Dr. Socol Agolli enjoying a brief respite
in Venice in the summer of 1993
from the arduous conditions at Tirana's
No.2 Hospital.*

FT:
*r. Linda Ciu is Albania's
ding paediatrician. Her
eciality is 'new borns' and the
sociated problems and she is
ad of the Neonatal Intensive
re Unit at the University
ternity Hospital of Tirana.
ring the past 10 years she
s trained all over the world
d particularly enjoyed her
ne in London where she
died at Gt. Ormond Street
ildren's Hospital. To
untless Albanian doctors, she
s been inspirational both in
r clinical expertise and her
alty to her country.
FA' is pleased to have
pplied her clinic with 3 infant
ntilators saving in total more
an 300 premature babies'
es a year.*

*ABOVE:
Klodian Karaj, age 5, miraculously
had the sight restored in his left eye
by the surgical team from the New
Victoria Hospital in Kingston-upon-
Thames.*

79

their own specialist fields, for doctors nationwide.

As for Anila, fate had yet another surprise in store. Thanks to the Trojan efforts of a Good Samaritan, Mrs. Barbara Locke, Anila has been brought to England for a 'lengthy' holiday and appears to be settling in wonderfully well in the Norfolk village of Attleborough. She has been attending Clare School in Norwich and now has a good command of the English language.

The author, far right, with Dr. Lindita Agolli, Dr. Linda Ciu and Prof. Sulejman Zhugli at Heathrow Airport in September 1992 after spending 3 weeks at London's top teaching hospitals. Having experienced the latest medical technology, the sadness showed on their faces at the thought of returning to the primitve conditions and frustration that awaited them in Tirana.

On the down side, Moorfields have diagnosed retinal detachments giving cause for major concern and it was discovered she was also deaf. That in part has been rectified by the use of a hearing aid.

No one knows just how old Anila Petrit Bido is, but she is thought to be about eighteen years old. Without doubt, she has suffered more in her relatively short life than most.

If it hadn't been for Bill Hamilton's BBC film, watched by millions and responsible for stirring Barbara Locke into action, Anila would still be languishing in Shkodra's home for mentally handicapped children.

Locked in an asylum with a group of unwanted children for fourteen years. Sitting and sleeping on cold stone, excreta covered, floors – deaf and blind and wrongly diagnosed as having a mental disability.

Thank God for people like Barbara Locke. She gave Anila a most precious gift – a chance. There are no bars on Barbara's windows and Anila's life here in rural England has been enriched beyond her wildest dreams. She has found something that has eluded her since the day of her illegitimate birth. For the first time, *she has found love*.

October 1991

Shkodra to Attleborough

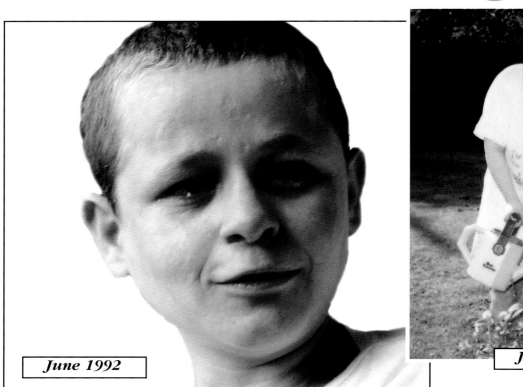

June 1992

82

August 1994

The incredible journey of Anila Petrit Bido

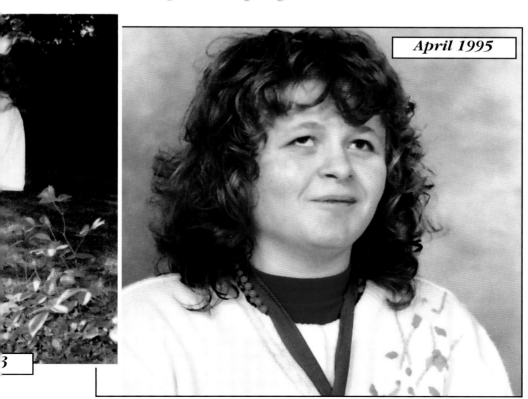

April 1995

6
THE FOURTEENTH MISSION AND THE DUCHESS OF YORK

T he BBC's graphic report of the appalling conditions at a second home for mentally handicapped children in the city of Berat brought an enormous response from the British public and offers of aid and help poured in from all quarters.

The Duchess of York's office at Buckingham Palace contacted the BBC and a meeting was hurriedly convened at the request of the Duchess herself. 'TFA' attended as did John Arthur of ADRA.

'Fergie' as she is affectionally known to millions was extremely concerned with the plight of these poor children and expressed a desire to come with us on our next trip, leaving on October 2nd.

'TFA' had despatched three, thirty-eight tonne trucks via Bari, two of which had been sent to the North Eastern town of Kruma at the personal request of Dr. Sali Berisha.

All the nurses at the Dystrophic Hospital thought the Duchess was absolutely wonderful.

The last stage of the journey. Officials from Kruma Town Council come to meet the trucks and are pictured here offering heartfelt thanks to Alan Bristow of 'TFA' and Rotary G.B. for sending humanitarian aid.

On board were almost one thousand boxes provided by Rotary International as part of their emergency relief scheme and each box, a virtual survival kit for a family of four, contained food, winter clothing, a medical kit and essential tools. Major problems were encountered by our man in the field, Alan Bristow, with adverse weather conditions preventing both vehicles from reaching their destination. They made it as far as Kukes and an alternative plan was put into operation, whereby, twelve smaller trucks arrived from Kruma, the aid transferred on the roadside, and then on to the desperate people of that region. The following day, a message of gratitude was received in Tirana from the Mayor of Kruma. The folk were thrilled as it was the first humanitarian aid ever received in that remote area.

The third truck made its way to Berat where equipment, including a scanner was unloaded at the hospital. As the children, fortunately, had been taken out of the 'Berat Home' and relocated in better accommodation, there was no point putting aid into an empty shell, so next stop was the mentally handicapped institution at Vlora. Finally, after 'overnighting' at a safe compound in Tirana, the truck arrived at 'TFA's compound in the Northern town of Bajze where it was unloaded and the aid distributed to the towns of Hani Hotit and Tomara.

Also on board were sixty boxes of vital supplies from Mother Teresa's 'Missionaries of Charity' in London for the home in Shkodra. These were delivered without a hitch as were twenty cots, to Shkodra's 'Teufik G'yli' orphanage.

Back in Tirana, 'TFA' succeeded to rendezvous with the Duchess of York at the Dystrophic hospital and aid in the form of cots, sheets, blankets and baby clothes collected by her charity 'Children in Crisis', was delivered by 'TFA'. It was great to see two British charities working together in harmony and it was immediately apparent, when one saw the Duchess cuddling those tiny babies, covered in ulcerated sores, just how much she cared.

On a different front but equally important; was 'TFA's meeting with the Minister of Defence Mr. Safet Zhulali. A request was put to him for two things. Firstly, a permanent warehouse in Tirana was needed, guarded twenty-four hours a day and preferably on military property under his direct control.

The second requirement was a number of soldiers to guard, load and unload the trucks at various locations.

We didn't have to wait long for his answer. "You shall have them both, and you have my word on that."

Now the real work could begin.

The Duchess of York with the author at Tirana's Dystrophic Hospital

7
THE ALBANIAN SYNDROME

I n Chapter Two, 'The Visit', mention was made briefly to The Albanian Syndrome (TAS), a most contagious, habit - forming affliction, that can strike at any time, but usually preys on those visiting Albania for the first time.

The incubation period has been known to last as long as three months but more often than not, symptoms appear within the first week of leaving the country. Aid workers, regardless of nationality or gender have continually fallen foul to this enigma. Indeed, the body's immune system appears quite incapable of protecting the victim from further attacks. Recent research recommended 'measured compliance' to be considered as an acceptable alternative treatment for 'TAS'.

It was in October 1991, on my first visit to Albania that I was affected by 'TAS' quite badly, but I think the reader is entitled to a more rational explanation of this strange phenomenon. From the moment I stepped off the aeroplane, I was surrounded by *'chaos'*. Others may have described it as 'a culture shock', but that was really the understatement of the year!

Everything was an unmitigated 'mess'.

Allow me to give the reader the 'briefest of insights'. Disembarking from the aircraft was a grim affair. At best it was hazardous, at worst it had close associations with 'Seppuku', more recently known as 'Hara Kiri' (stomach cutting), the Japanese ritual of suicide. The passengers did have a choice, jump the twenty feet onto the runway or jump the two feet gap onto the rickety steps that had been pushed into place by ten, rather shady looking individuals. We chose the latter.

Immigration was a nightmare. Customs clearance was non-existent. Had a bomb been smuggled in, with hindsight, I think the Albanian authorities would have welcomed it. It may have made discernible improvements.

The road to Tirana, some fifteen miles distant, was peppered with a million potholes. Driving over one was sufficient to bring on an instant attack of 'sciatica' to the owner of even the strongest back – that is of course, providing a vehicle was available!

In Tirana, conditions were deplorable. No shops, no money, no work, no transport, no food, no clothing, no water, no electricity and no hope.

A total breakdown of the infrastructure had taken place. The basement of the prestigious Tirana Hotel was awash with untreated sewage and with electricity available for only two hours a day, it could hardly get worse.

The hospitals were the final straw and the underlying cause of a recurrent nightmare that would haunt me for months to come. I had a real fear of being *'taken ill'* and my dream was of waking up in hospital only to be told that the infection in my right foot had spread, so the doctors had no choice but to amputate my leg!

I couldn't take any more, I had to get away – I needed to escape.

Returning to England, I resumed my normal life. I was safe, happy, yet it all seemed terribly 'mundane' after Albania. I didn't know it then, but I was in the first throes of The Albanian Syndrome. I was actually *'missing'* the chaos and confusion, experiencing the most profound withdrawal symptoms and each time I went to Albania and returned, it was exactly the same.

As conditions in the country improved, so the effects of 'TAS' receded. Now it's gone completely and in a quiet moment, I wonder if it really happened at all – perhaps I imagined the whole thing.........

8

THE SIXTEENTH MISSION

O n this occasion, I was accompanied by Michael Randall whose assistance proved to be invaluable and was very much appreciated.

Back in November 1993 'TFA' had deposited fifty tonnes of aid in a state warehouse in Durres for the first time. Every assurance was given by the Director of State Reserves Mr. Hekuran Skuqi that it would be under constant guard and on our return in February 1994 would be just as we had left it.

A tall order indeed.

It was with a certain amount of trepidation that we watched the giant padlocks being unlocked, the doors rolled back and to our delight, everything was there and intact.

Twelve, seven and a half tonne army trucks arrived courtesy of the Ministry of Defence and the six hour loading operation began. By 3.00 p.m. it was completed and escorted by eight police officers, the convoy moved out of 'reserva shteterore' and began the three and a half hour journey to the northern city of Shkodra.

The aid is safe and the loading begins.

The military convoy en route to Shkodra.

The author, Luketa Hasa and the pupils of Bajze's middle school.

A warehouse had been made available by our good friend Mr. Ali Spahia and within two hours of arrival in Shkodra, every item was unloaded and safely stored, ready for delivery the next day. Twenty five tonnes would go to the people of Shkodra whilst the remainder would be distributed to the surrounding villages.

It had been the first time we had involved the Military and a Government agency in our operation and it worked extremely well. Large trucks are needed to take the aid from the UK to Albania but once there, they are of little use in transporting it to outlying towns and villages. Mountain roads are bad, full of potholes and often have very low bridges, making it impossible for large vehicles to pass. This new system of using smaller army trucks, loading from a central warehouse close to the docks,

Michael Randall relaxes with his good friend Prof. Sulejman Zhugli.

seemed to be the way forward.

After spending a most enjoyable night as the guests of Luketa and Marion Hasa in Bajze, we were escorted to the middle school to meet the Mayor, Mr. Gjek Malaj, together with the school's headmaster Mr. Tom Asllani and the Member of Parliament for the Great Highlands Mr. Dode Kacaj.

During the past two years 'TFA' has spent a lot of time in and around Bajze and we have got to know the people very well indeed. They are wonderful folk, without doubt the kindest people we've ever met. Simple, poor, yet incredibly generous with what little they have. After a brief but moving ceremony for which the whole town turned out, the school was renamed 'John van Weenen'. A far cry from its old name 'Communist Hero'. I left feeling very humble to have been honoured in such a way.

That afternoon we returned to Shkodra to visit the 'Teufik G'yli' orphanage to assess the children's needs. The orphanage was finding it almost impossible to get medicines from the hospital and desperately needed antibiotics. A list was prepared and enquiries initiated to gather such essentials in time for the May trip.

Finally, there was the visit to the home in Durres of Arben and Mimoza Nexhipi whose baby daughter Jessica had been the inspiration for the formation of 'TFA'. Although Jessica had died, Mimoza had given birth to another daughter whose names Antonia Joy were chosen by the pupils of Kingsbrook School in Bedford.

Upon entering the Nexhipis' squalid one-room flat, we were appalled to see Mimoza eight and a half months pregnant again. They were penniless with no income whatsoever and Arben who suffered from tuberculosis, had never even heard of condoms or birth control. Mimoza, in tears, pleaded for my help. "My baby will be born in two weeks time and I have no milk in my breasts – what shall I do?"

Arrangements were made to have powdered baby milk delivered weekly until we returned again with fresh supplies. The team also planned to disinfect and decorate the Nexhipis' home and if it was not too presumptuous, offer some sound advice on family planning.

Brave smiles for the camera conceal the heartache and tragedy of the Nexhipi family.

The last person you see when you leave Albania's Rinas Airport – File, the baggage handler, who cuddles everyone in sight.

93

9

THE SEVENTEENTH MISSION

S tarting on 3rd May 1994, it was to prove the most difficult trip since the original excursion some twenty-seven months earlier. Fortunately, the team selected to go, had experience in the field, a factor that would figure highly in the ultimate success of the mission.

Two juggernaut trucks, packed to capacity with clothing and medical supplies, had been dispatched from Northamptonshire three days earlier and sailing on the Bari ferry, arrived safely at Durres on Wednesday 4th May. The team comprising Alan Bristow, Azad Kumar, Alan Blake, Bernard Coppen and myself flew out with Austrian Airlines, arriving in good time to meet the trucks at Durres docks.

Left to right: Azad Kumar, Alan Blake, Alan Bristow and Bernard Coppen.

Armed police on guard at the Bajze warehouse. Were they there solely to protect 'TFA's aid shipments or was there something more sinister?

It was 9.30 p.m. before the overzealous and bureaucratic customs officers allowed the vehicles to pass into the country and four hours of hard night driving later, our police escorted convoy arrived at 'TFA's

Looking across the magnificent 'Great Highlands' of Albania, Vermosh, to the far north, looks a long way off indeed.

This little mountain boy stares in bewilderment after been given sweets for the first time.

warehouse at Bajze. The truck drivers 'opted' to sleep in their cabs, leaving the team to grab a few hours sleep before the arrival of ten military trucks at 10.00 a.m. the following morning.

By midday there was no sign of them and eight hours later, they still had not materialised. Telephoning Tirana to see if they had left would seem to be the answer. Just one small problem with that idea – there were no telephones.

At 10.00 p.m. that night, ten huge army trucks rolled into Bajze. The team just looked at one another and didn't say a word – the relief over their arrival spoke volumes.

Unloading and reloading began at first light and by 11.00 a.m. on Friday morning the military convoy moved out of Bajze and headed northwards into the rugged mountains of Malsia e Madhe, the Great Highlands.

Dode Kacaj, Member of

His sister wonders if there might be some for her – and there were.

Vermosh Hospital, now just a bare, empty shell, after being vandalised by the communists in early 1991, when they realised they were losing control.

Parliament for Malsia e Madhe, had selected ten remote villages, spread over a vast area, where little or no aid had gone before. Eight trucks would cover the Kelmendi region taking aid to the far north close to the border with Montenegro. Every person in the villages of Vermosh, Lepusha, Selca, Tomara, Broja, Kozhnje, Vulke and Nikci received 'something'. The two remaining trucks headed into the region of Kastrat, to the villages of Bratoshe and Kastrat.

The whole operation lasted two days and surprisingly, went like clockwork. Exhausted, the team returned to Bajze and delivered fifty boxes of clothes to the town's middle school. Later, the headmaster, Mr.

The long journey to the Kelmendi region begins.

Tom Asllani, reported that every one of the four hundred children had been clothed. Forty boxes of general medical supplies were also taken to Bajze's medical centre and the clinic's resident doctor, over a glass of 'Raki,' was overheard saying, "Christmas in May – how wonderful."

After a good night's sleep aided by a generous flow of 'Raki' an early start was made for Shkodra and the much awaited visit to 'Teufik G'yli' our favourite orphanage. Seeing the children again was for us, a great pleasure and watching

File Vushaj of Vermosh in full traditional highland dress.

them change into the new clothes we had brought for them was a marvellous experience. Becoming attached, for both parties, is inevitable and although the oldest is only eight years old, they do not get upset when we leave, for they know, in a short while, we will be back.

Driving out of Shkodra, one cannot fail to be impressed by the ruins of Rozafa Castle sitting high above the city. We drove up the winding road, through the old wooden gates and into the castle grounds. It was a warm sunny day with a gentle breeze and the castle was completely deserted.

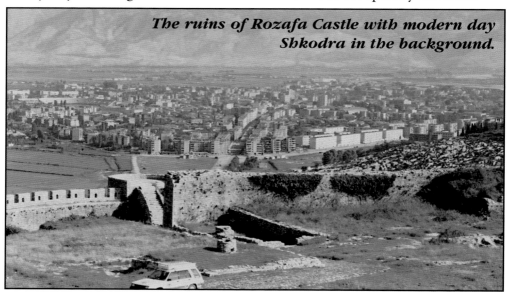

The ruins of Rozafa Castle with modern day Shkodra in the background.

The panoramic view across the Plain of Shkodra to the south and the mountains of Malsia e Madhe to the north was quite incredible. To the west lay the Lake of Shkodra, as calm as a mill pond, stretching lazily, and disappearing from view in the midday heat haze to the border with Montenegro. Sitting there, so peaceful, one could almost hear the voices of the Illyrians who had come three thousand years before to lay the first stones. It brought to mind one of Albania's most famous folk stories, the Legend of Rozafa after whom the castle was named.

'The Legend of Immurement' tells the story of three brothers, all stonemasons who set to work building the castle. However, the walls that were erected by day, were mysteriously shattered by night. A wise old man advised the brothers to make a human sacrifice, so they decided to immure one of their wives in the castle wall. Whichever wife brought the brothers their meal the next morning would be the one

A smiling Mimoza Nexhipi with baby Jenny.

99

Rozafa – immured forever in the castle walls.

and they gave their word of honour to each other not to say anything of this matter to their wives. Only the youngest brother kept his promise and in the morning, when the two older women refused to take breakfast to the brothers, the younger woman did so.

There she learned of her destiny and accepted their decision but was extremely saddened at the thought of leaving her little boy, who was just a baby. Rozafa was convinced the sacrifice was best for her tribe and before dying told the masons this:

"When I am immured in the walls, let out the right side of my body. My right arm to hold my little son, my right eye to see him and my right breast to suckle him."

The legend tells how the castle remained standing as her blood cemented the walls and her milk continued to flow until the child was older. After her death, there remained on the walls a white spot, that can be seen even to this day.

It was late on Sunday when the team left Rozafa Castle and began the three hour drive back to Tirana via Lezhe, Laç and Kruje.

The following day, at 7.30 a.m. sharp we headed for Durres to visit, as promised, the Nexhipi family. We took food and clothing and much needed powdered baby milk for Mimosa's new baby. She was ecstatic, after all – her baby was going to live, and would not share the same fate as her first child Jessica, who died of malnutrition.

Back in Tirana the rest of the day would be taken up with meetings and making arrangements for future trips. Task Force Albania had been operating now for two and a half years and had come to a crossroads.

In September 1991, food was the priority with many people dying of starvation. It took a year for that situation to change and with the fall of communism and democratic elections, agricultural land in rural areas was given back to people to grow their own crops. The following year, the emphasis had switched to clothing, bedding and general medical supplies. The story now moves to May 1994.

'TFA' had been considering building a Medical Centre/Hospital in northern Albania and this trip enabled a feasibility study to be carried out. After detailed discussions with President Berisha, the Ministry of Health and many senior doctors, it became obvious that this idea would not be in the country's best interest.

Tirana Hospital, most of all, needs medical equipment, and only in the capital, is there the expertise to use it. The system is so structured, that if people are seriously ill, they visit Tirana. There is no sense at all putting sophisticated equipment into remote hospitals where it will never be used because the doctors are not trained in its practical application.

The Medical Centre was losing credibility fast. Something of a romantic notion – perhaps a dream, and that's what it would remain. The simple truth was the people on the ground knew far better than us just what was needed.

As we left Eduart Selami's office in the Democratic Party building the following morning and crossed Skanderbeg Square for the last time on that trip, we noticed something quite different.

Gone were the hordes of faceless people walking aimlessly with nowhere to go, that we had seen in October 1991. Gone too, were the countless numbers whose eyes had no hope – and in their place, were different people. They walked with confidence – with purpose. They knew where they were going. The square bristled with activity, and cars, unknown in earlier times, were everywhere. Uncannily, in that fleeting moment, we had all shared the same thought. The long night of communism was over and we were witnessing a new day dawning in Albania's history.

It was not necessary to speak. We all felt very privileged being part of it.

The formidable and beautiful Great Highlands of Albania.

10
THE PILOTS

On 24th December 1944, a light aircraft left an airfield near Bari in southern Italy. Its destination was Garon in Montenegro. On board the plane were three men, all thought to be pilots and the flight path would take them across the Adriatic Sea in a northerly direction.

The first land they sighted was the southern tip of Montenegro followed by the Lake of Shkodra. Interestingly enough, the border between the former Yugoslavia and Albania runs exactly through the centre of the lake.

The route now lay across the formidable mountains of Malsia e Madhe (The Great Highlands) to the most northerly point of Albania. The weather was bad, visibility poor and the pilot had no radar to assist him. With peaks in the region rising to eleven thousand feet, they had to gain as much altitude as possible. The next day was Christmas Day and no doubt the men were in jubilant mood. Beside them lay large sacks of Christmas mail, eagerly awaited by friends and relatives just over the border in Montenegro.

The tiny village of Tomara lay behind them now, nestling in a craggy gorge and the whole landscape was covered in snow. The single road, visible until late September, had vanished and heavy snow drifts could be seen intermittently through the dark massing clouds.

As they negotiated the mountain range on the eastern side of the village of Vermosh, the weather closed in. A blinding snowstorm cut visibility to zero and an eye witness recounted how five thousand feet below, he caught sight momentarily of a small aircraft being tossed around – then it was gone.

There was only one peak in front of them, after which, the border with Montenegro lay just five miles away, virtually 'downhill and plain sailing'.

From what took place in the next few minutes, we must assume the pilot thought he had gained sufficient altitude to clear the last obstacle. He hadn't.

Marj Booya's father witnessed the crash briefly catching sight of the plane as it flew straight into the mountain, close to the peak. The snow was so thick, the aircraft just impacted itself into the mountainside. The fuselage protruded horizontally and remained in that position until the following spring when it broke away as the snow melted and plunged two thousand feet into a ravine.

When Booya's father reached the original crash site, he found two bodies lying in the snow. They were surrounded by hundreds of Christmas cards. He buried the two pilots in a hillside grave with all reverence. The communist officials who forcibly accompanied him, confiscated the pilots' personal belongings. All he could salvage for himself was a sheepskin flying jacket and a pair of opera glasses.

It was now May 1945 and the war in Europe was over. The following week, he made his way to the aircraft's final resting place and there, in the battered shell, discovered a third body. He buried the man in a shallow grave and marked the spot with a headstone.

Three years later, his son was born and in 1955 when he was seven years old he took him to the two sites and showed him the three graves. His father had told him the two pilots who were buried at the top of the mountain were English and an initial story I had heard implied the plane was a Spitfire. As I understand it, most Spitfires were single seaters but a number of twin seaters were manufactured towards the end of the war. If there are three bodies, then it definitely was not a Spitfire and the pilots may not have been English.

That is the story so far – however . . .

_____

'TFA's 17th mission took place in May 1994, and with me on that trip were Alan Bristow, Alan Blake, Azad Kumar and Bernard Coppen. We had covered most of the villages in the Kelmendi region and on the night of 5th May were staying with a Vermosh family and local mayor Jek Alia.

In the course of conversation at dinner, the 'story' of the crashed plane surfaced. Needless to say, we were all fascinated, as our original information had come from an entirely different source. Until this point, there had never been a scrap of proof to suggest the story was true.

All eyes turned to an eighteen year old boy seated at the table, whom, we were told was the grandson of the man who found the plane in 1944. "Have you anything from the plane?" I asked. "Yes," came the answer, "I have a pair of binoculars."

Ten minutes later, the boy burst into the room. He was clutching what turned out to be a pair of opera glasses. They were quite old, made of brass and heavily dented and on the top was written 'Le Jockey Club – Paris'. "My father can tell you more." "Where is he?" I asked. "At home," replied the boy. "Shall I get him?" "Yes please!" we all replied in unison. Five minutes later Marj Booya strode into the room. Two more bottles of 'Raki' appeared and Booya began his story.

His father had indeed found the plane, had a confrontation with the communist authorities and buried three pilots, two at the top and one in a ravine.

After his initial trip with his father at the age of seven, Booya had returned to the graves many times, knew exactly where they were – and could show us! "Thank you very much," I said, "that's wonderful."

"Apart from the opera glasses, was there anything else found?" "Yes," said Booya, "there was a flying jacket and it's here – or was in Vermosh. My father gave it to his friend who lives three miles down the valley." It was now 11.00 p.m. and 'as black as the ace of spades' outside. "We'll go at first light."

Our host cleared away the table and the empty glasses whilst the women made up eight beds on the floor. We quickly fell asleep, full of anticipation, knowing the dawn would come very soon.

At 4.00 a.m. it did. We rose, put on our shoes and filed quietly out of the house. No one spoke. It was barely light. We walked for a mile along the river before crossing it on stepping stones and headed up into a forest. The going was very tough and we found it difficult to keep up with Nikolin Narkaj and Marj Booya. George Hysaj brought up the rear. One and a half hours later we arrived at the house. Booya knocked at the door – it was 5.30 a.m. Everyone was asleep – except us.

While we waited for a reply, I thought, "Is this really happening? Suppose it was my house in England and eight men were knocking on the door at 5.30 a.m. and when I opened it, they informed me they wanted a flying jacket given to my father by his friend in December 1944 – fifty-one years ago!"

Probably I would think they were mad!

The door opened. After a few words from Booya we were ushered into the house. There was only one room, in which the family slept by night and lived by day. Out came the 'Raki.' The story was repeated once more and a middle aged man disappeared into the rear of the house. He returned clutching an oil-skin. "Is this what you are looking for?" he asked. "No," I replied, as he handed me the oilskin. I thanked him very much anyway and was about to hand it back to him, when something made me stop. The oilskin was so heavy – how could that be? It certainly didn't look very thick.

Within everyone's view, I turned it inside out and there sewn into the oilskin as a lining, was the sheepskin flying jacket!

Pandemonium broke out as we searched for identifying names and numbers - there was nothing. The lady of the house came over and cut the stitching and insisted we take it as a present. With some reluctance we did so but not before assuring her we would take it to London for an examination after which we would return it to her.

Within three days we were back in England certain of one thing. The plane did exist, it was not just a story and we had in our possession the pilots' binoculars and flying jacket.

The Flying Jacket.

Whatever happened, we all knew one thing was certain – we would find the plane and in turn discover the identity of the pilots, and if they had surviving children, we would find them and inform them of how their fathers died. Most of all, at long last, they could be given a proper religious burial.

That was the story – so far.

Alan Bristow had accompanied me yet again on this the 22nd mission and when I asked him why he kept returning (and at considerable expense to himself), he shook his head and replied "I just love the place".

Mark Seabrook, the husband of Elaine who had been a member on the

Mark Seabrook in reflective mood.

21st trip, was experiencing Albania for the first time.

Arriving in Tirana on Tuesday 27th July 1995, we had completed our work which included the delivery and installation of an infant ventilator in Tirana's Maternity Hospital. This was the second of three that we planned to install, but at twenty thousand dollars each, the cost was considerable.

Had it not been for the intervention of John McGough, representing the S.L.E. Corporation of England, 'TFA's infant ventilator programme' would not have been possible.

John McGough is a forty-nine year old American married with one lovely child and resident in Hungary. For a living he sells medical appliances to all and sundry and is presently employed by the S.L.E. Corporation of South Croydon in Surrey.

The reader could be forgiven for thinking, "What's so special about a salesman?" So I offer a word of caution – "This is no ordinary salesman." Read on.

I first met John 'McGo,' as the Albanians call him in October 1992. He'd had a reasonable week remuneratively speaking, having just sold seventeen ventilators to John Arthur of the ADRA organisation. John McGough indeed was 'a man of many parts,' as I was about to find out. He was the Eastern European representative for S.L.E. International, a position surely enhanced by being the Albanian Consul in Switzerland. With a distinguished military record, including service in Vietnam, John McGough even persuaded the Albanian Airforce to put at his disposal a Chinese made helicopter gunship.

The ex-Chinese helicopter gunship landing at Lushnje.

To the aid agencies like ADRA, this method of transport, dropping vital medical aid directly into remote mountain village hospitals was like 'manna from heaven.' Watching him operate for the first time was a sobering experience – I felt quite useless!

I had been waiting along with Bill Hamilton and John Arthur at the Tirana military airfield for our versatile pilot to appear. The green Chinese monster was loaded with ventilators, fuelled and ready to go. It seemed half the Albanian Airforce were on parade awaiting his arrival.

A car drew up, a junior officer opened the rear door and out stepped John McGough. The assembled officers saluted him. Everything appeared satisfactory and he returned the salute.

The super salesman was wearing what became known as 'his Vietnamese outfit'. He took control immediately. The high ranking officers present seemed terribly impressed by the number of 'badges' displayed on J.M.'s uniform. I think in retrospect, they saw him as a cross between a saviour and Ghenghis Khan.

Within minutes pilot McGough was at the helm, we were airborne and heading for the city of Lushnje.

Lt. Col. John McGough – the pilot.

Circling the city twice, (for maximum effect), he landed close to the hospital. As the multitudes closed in, J.M. appeared on the bridge and addressed his people.

The ecstatic children of Lushnje crowd round with two finger gestures depicting the Democratic Party's slogan of 'freedom and democracy'.

Many of the assembled crowd had never seen a helicopter in their lives before. Some assumed Albania had been selected as the site for *an alien invasion* whilst others remarked in a rather blasé way, that they never expected *'God'* to turn up in a green Chinese helicopter gunship!

His address was magnificent. Then, with ventilator and entourage in tow, he headed towards the hospital but not before unbuttoning his flying suit, removing it to display underneath, a white technician's jacket.

Once inside the hospital, he carried out his role as technical consultant, first assembling the machine and then conducting a thirty minute seminar in maintenance for four bewildered engineers.

Lastly, he gathered all the relevant doctors together for an explanation of operating procedures but only after taking off his white technician's jacket, pulling a long white doctor's coat from inside his trousers, allowing it to fall free and attaching the customary stethoscope.

Voilà! Our chameleon friend had changed yet again, this time – into a medic! An hour later, back at the helicopter he was giving his final address to the assembled throng. They loved him.

John Arthur of ADRA thought he was wonderful. The charity's ventilator was installed and attached to a patient. The hospital technicians thought he was out of this world, (some of us thought that might not be a bad place for him to go!) The doctors, with the latest piece of western technology would become miracle workers and the people had been inspired by J.M.'s words of wisdom.

Everyone was a winner.

As he donned his 'Vietnamese outfit' once more, turned and gave a

very last wave to his people, perhaps I could be forgiven for imagining I detected the wry smile of a salesman who had just closed the sale satisfactorily. I knew it would be just the first of many.

Which brings me back to Saturday 1st July 1995 when John McGough, through the Ministry of Health, had

Left:
John McGough, the world's greatest salesman (so he tells us) and few would disagree.

arranged for a helicopter to take us to Vermosh to search for the graves of the three pilots.

Stephen Nash, the British chargé d'affaires had come to see us off. John had to return to Switzerland unexpectedly but provided us with two first class pilots. We had invited Dr. Roland Xhaxho for medical reasons, should we be successful in finding the graves and exhuming the bodies.

The journey to Vermosh took about one hour and took in some spectacular scenery. George Hysaj, chairman of the Democratic Party was there to meet us along with Marj Booya whose father found the crashed aircraft in May 1945.

Below:
Our good friend Dr. Roland Xhaxho.

The plan was to fly to the top of the mountain where the two pilots were buried. The helicopter would make two trips as there were eleven of us.

Although it was July, many of the mountains still had snow on them but the pilot fortunately found a grassy plateau to land on.

It was hot and the air was clear. Far below, the small scattered town of Vermosh stretched lazily almost out of sight to the mountains of

The author with Alan Bristow at the grave site.

Marj Booya, whose father reached the crashed aircraft in May 1945.

Montenegro. Wild flowers abounded everywhere, buttercups, forget-me-nots and wild orchids swayed gently in the breeze.

Booya explained the grave lay about half a mile away and it would take us the best part of a hour to get there. It was not an easy walk but we finally arrived at the grave site.

The two pilots had been buried on the top of a hill, two hundred yards above the spot where the plane had crashed. There were two small white rocks surrounded by long coarse tufty grass.

The ex-Swiss Army, now Albanian Ministry of Health helicopter, landing safely on top of the mountain.

"This is the place," said Booya.

It was a strange moment indeed, the assembly of eleven men stood in a circle around the grave. I offered a small prayer and instinctively everyone bowed their heads. Religious denominations (and there were many represented there) were unimportant. Each man stood in humility, alone and with his own thoughts.

After a few moments, there followed a discussion between the Albanians and then Booya, George and a third man began digging. It was a shallow grave, therefore not long before bones started to appear.

In fifty one years, the two bodies had decomposed completely. All that was left were bones. The two men had been buried side by side in a single coffin, which had obviously rotted. Soon, all the remains of the two pilots had been removed but unfortunately, there were no signs of any dog tags or numbers of any description. Their nationality remained a mystery.

The grave, marked by two white stones where the two pilots were buried fifty years ago.

Tradition in Malsia e Madhe dictated that once a body had been disturbed, it could not be put back in the same ground, so the pilots' remains were carefully put into a box and

George Hysaj (left) and Marj Booya (right) flank two Vermosh officials after exhuming the remains of the two pilots.

113

taken back to the helicopter.

An hour later we landed back at Vermosh, said goodbye to our Albanian friends and headed for Tirana.

Stephen Nash, the British chargé d'affaires, took charge of the pilots' remains and asked us to notify the Commonwealth War Graves Commission and the Ministry of Defence of events that had taken place, when we got back to England. This we did.

The crashed aircraft lies two thousand feet below the grave in a deep ravine. Most of the year it is covered in snow. We were told that during the following September when our next mission was planned the plane would be accessible. So at the time of writing, August 1995, we still did not know the pilots' nationality. Until we do, no graves can be commemorated, either in Albania or elsewhere.

The one thing we now know for certain is that in 1944 a light aircraft did crash and the countless stories told to us over several years, were true.

Perhaps one day in the not too distant future, an unknown man or woman will learn of their father's fate and the uncertainty that has endured all these years over his disappearance will be ended.

The story moves on . . .

More determined than ever to discover the identity of the third pilot, we returned to Vermosh as planned in September 1995.

John McGough's friend and fellow pilot Cenan flew us out once more to the very most northern tip of Albania. On board was Alan Blake, Azad Kumar, Tim Eyrl our intrepid cameraman, who had gone to film the event for posterity and finally, myself.

The crashed aircraft had been released from the thawing snow in May 1945 and hurled two thousand feet down the mountainside into a ravine. Soon after, Marj Booya's father had visited the site in the hope of finding the third airman, which he did to his credit, and buried him in a shallow grave.

It was too far to climb up from the village, so we arranged for Cenan to fly above the ravine to a safe landing spot, where we alighted and began the one hour trek down the mountain.

The air was thin and the going hard but we eventually arrived at the place our Albanian guide thought we would find the aircraft remains. He

For fifty-three years, this seven cylinder rotary engine has lain in a deep crevice high up in the mountains of northern Albania. To this day it remains unidentified.

was right. There – jammed between two large rocks was an aircraft engine. On closer inspection we discovered it was a seven cylinder rotary engine with readable numbers stamped on all cylinder heads.

There was no name-plate on the engine or any clues of any kind as to the type or make of aircraft that it had once been part of. Combing the area, we found nothing else at all, but then, the incident had taken place fifty

Right:
A section of a cylinder head from the seven cylinder rotary engine.

115

years earlier and mother nature had been very busy in the interim period.

The guide unfortunately, did not know the whereabouts of the grave, so after taking photographs and recording any part numbers still visible, we began the long climb back up the mountain to where Cenan was waiting for us.

Within minutes it was obvious we were in trouble. The air was very thin indeed. First Tim fell to the ground and then I followed suit. It was as if my heart was outside my body – it was beating very loudly indeed. Never had I experienced such a sensation – it was frightening. Azad Kumar was having difficulty walking and was breathing very quickly. His head was covered with thousands of tiny droplets of perspiration. I remember them glistening in the late afternoon sun.

The helicopter was at least one and a half hours away and by the time we reached it, it would be nearly dark. Tim, Azad and myself just couldn't go on any further – we were *finished*.

The guide came back to see us and asked what was wrong. Fortunately for Anglo-Albanian relations, none of us could speak, otherwise the air may have been just a shade blue. The words just wouldn't come out – we were exhausted.

To our consternation, Alan Blake seemed totally unaffected by the high altitude and was jumping about like a spring lamb. This made us feel worse than ever. And to add insult to injury, the guide, whose movements resembled a cross between a mountain goat and an Afghan hound, was wearing carpet slippers!

Realising there was a serious problem, the guide said he would go and get the helicopter and Alan Blake decided to go with him. Thirty minutes later we could see two tiny figures disappearing over the mountain top to get help.

On the side of the mountain was a small flat area where previously a shepherd had herded his sheep. It was covered with large rocks so we cleared them very slowly and created a landing pad should Cenan be brave enough to risk it.

The sun was setting – it was turning colder and the wind was increasing. The thought of spending a night out there was unthinkable.

The silence was broken by the helicopter's engine, despite us not being able to see it. Suddenly, it was hovering overhead, the down draught was tremendous and we crawled away from the flat landing area.

Cenan tried to land but had to abort as the strong winds almost blew him into the mountainside. The door was open and on his second attempt, he made it onto the landing pad as we ran, heads down and clambered aboard. The rotor blade was only feet above the rock on one side and if a gust of wind had blown at that particular moment, it would certainly have been fatal.

Within seconds, Cenan pulled the helicopter up and outwards to safety. It was a brilliant piece of aviation although some of us were too ill to appreciate it at the time.

Vermosh could just be seen in the twilight, thousands of feet below and minutes later we were saying goodbye to our guide but not before an old man thrust a small metal capsule into my hand. I didn't know him – we didn't speak, but he thought I should have it.

Throughout the long one hour journey back to Tirana, no one spoke. We had been very lucky, or stupid, and perhaps with the pictures and engine numbers we might at last discover the nationality of the three pilots together with the make of the plane.

Surprisingly, RAF Innsworth in Gloucestershire could not help us at all

'The Cyanide Capsule'
The label around the capsule read as follows:
6 – Energy Tablets
Take only as instructed by Officer in command.

despite having given them a great deal of information. It may be just coincidence, but that small metal capsule was in fact a 'cyanide pill' with an interesting instruction on the side. Perhaps it may be nearer the truth that on that December night, over fifty years ago, a clandestine mission was in progress and to acknowledge it – even now, may cause embarrassment in certain quarters.

For now, the mountain must keep its secret, but it is only a matter of time . . .

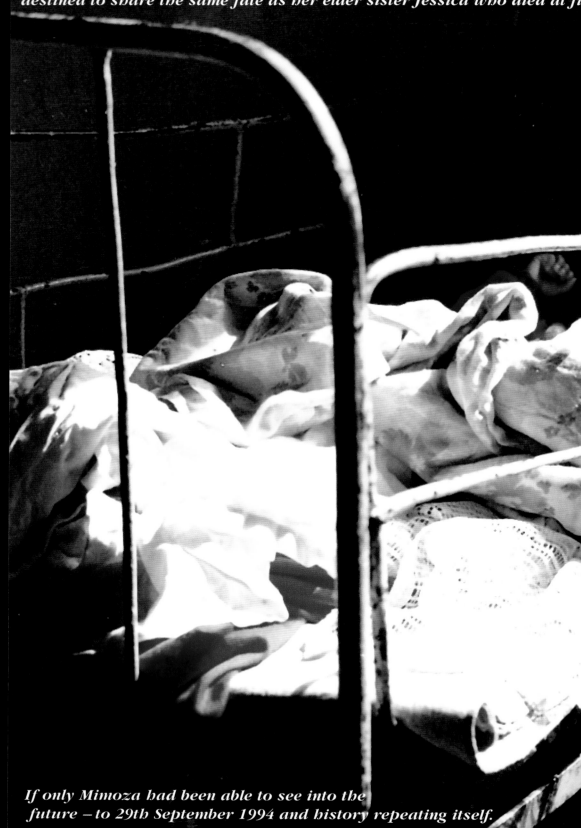

A shaft of sunlight penetrates the darkened room. Nine month old baby J[...]
remaining strength to peer through the bars of her rusted cot. Pneumoni[...]
destined to share the same fate as her elder sister Jessica who died at fi[...]

If only Mimoza had been able to see into the
future — to 29th September 1994 and history repeating itself.

...chipi musters all her ...ken its toll. She seemed ...s of malnutrition.

11
THE EIGHTEENTH MISSION

September 1994

President Berisha had expressed a wish that 'TFA' might like to concentrate its humanitarian aid efforts within the medical field.

At Tirana University Hospital, there remained a dire shortage of medical equipment in almost every department although, ironically, the expertise to use it was available.

With this in mind, veteran aid worker Roy Richards joined forces with Gordon Collis to accompany me on the trip and the fact that both were black belts in karate was most reassuring.

Teamwork is essential and dependability of its members vital, especially in times of confusion, when a situation can deteriorate so rapidly that within seconds an innocent crowd can become a mob. Unattended, a large truck laden with aid would not remain so for long. Despite any obvious appeal, the most mundane load could be quickly laundered into cash. Consequently, our security had remained tight, resulting in little having been stolen during the previous seventeen missions.

This time we had despatched two juggernauts to the Albanian port of Durres and once through customs, they were escorted safely on to Tirana

University Hospital. On board were sixty hydraulic hospital beds complete with mattresses and bedside cabinets all bound for the ophthalmological wards of No. 1 Hospital.

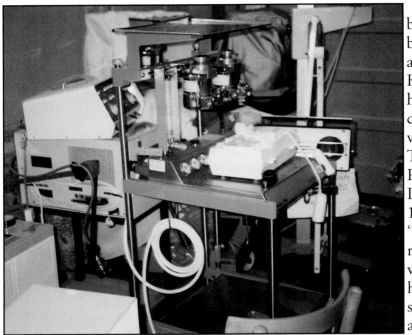

They had been donated by Dewsbury and Harrogate hospitals and came to us via Brian Thornton of Rotary International, 1040 District. 'TFA's relationship with Rotary had strengthened a great deal

Sophisticated medical equipment all donated free of charge.

during the previous twelve months and Brian deserved much of the credit for it. Somehow, he had collected, stored and then delivered the whole consignment to our warehouse in Peterborough – all with amazing efficiency.

Also on board were some very sophisticated pieces of medical apparatus donated by Community Hospitals Ltd of Pine Hill in Hitchin, Herts. Amongst the equipment were anaesthetic machines, visual field analysers, a dental X-ray unit, a dental steriliser, an ultra sonic body scanner and a heart monitor. The total value of the medical apparatus was in the vicinity of £200,000.

The next day we headed north to the town of Koplik and to a superb warehouse next door to

Right:
A pretty fair haired Albanian girl trying very hard to force a smile.

the police station. Koplik is the county town of Malsia e Madhe and lies twenty kilometres south of the border with Montenegro.

The Director of Education was there to meet us. He knew we had brought ten pallets of school equipment, enough to cover the needs, in the short term, of every child in northern Albania.

He became quite ecstatic at the sight of literally millions of exercise books, pens, pencils and rubbers, etc. That consignment alone was worth an estimated £50,000.

For some time now 'TFA' had desperately needed a van large enough to transport aid to remote areas that larger trucks could not negotiate. I had approached all the major British manufacturers but to no avail. A second-hand vehicle would be fine but it would have to be acquired free of charge. One disinterested garage owner protested "You must be joking" although in his defence, offered personally to "have me committed".

Finally I turned to my then local garage at Collyweston near Stamford in Lincolnshire and the owners, Bob and Don Close went out and bought a superb low mileage Mazda E2000 van. They serviced it at no cost and arranged for Barker Signs at Casterton to

The stench from the excreta was unbearable but this sad little Albanian boy hadn't even noticed it.

signwrite it, again at no cost, for which we are very grateful to Malcolm as indeed we are to Collyweston Garage, as it's the second vehicle they have given us.

The Mazda van was driven on board one of the trucks, having first been filled to capacity with new clothes for the orphaned children of Shkodra. These were delivered safely following a brief visit to Mother Teresa's Home nearby, where ten large Rotary boxes were deposited with the sisters for distribution.

Back in Tirana, it was most encouraging to see all the new hospital beds in place, complete with bedside cabinets, together with an increase

Gordon Collis from Bedfordshire shares the happiness of the orphaned children from Shkodra as they proudly show off their new clothes from England.

in morale amongst the doctors and nurses. Our relatively limited efforts were making a difference but there was still a long way to go.

The charity owed a great deal to Baroness Chalker, the Overseas Development Minister and to Peter Burton at the ODA for their support and assistance in securing a £25,000 grant to cover transport costs, without which 'TFA' could not have continued its aid programme.

Being isolated for forty-seven years from the rest of the world had taken its toll, but it had not killed the people's spirit.

Subjected to the most ruthless totalitarian regime ever known under the dictatorship of Enver Hoxha had not extinguished the flame of freedom completely. With every passing day, that flame grows brighter, and now, several years after the first free and fair elections, and a landslide win for the Democratic Party, the ghost of Albania's Stalinist past has finally been laid to rest.

It's either this – or walk.

12
THE CRUCIFIX

Midway between Tirana and the northern city of Shkodra lies the town of Lezhe with a population of some twelve thousand people. On our journeys north, it developed into almost a ritual for us to stop just south of the town at a rather attractive little roadside cafe.

The owner's name was Agron, a most amenable chap who, whenever he saw our red Mazda van approaching, ran out into the street and physically welcomed us with open arms, as if we were his close relatives returning from the dead.

His modest establishment had no gas or electricity whatsoever, yet his one 'claim to fame' was his amazing ability to produce at will, ice cold Coca-Colas. It took us a while to discover just how he did it.

Directly behind the cafe was a 'mountain range.' Concealed in its base was a tiny wooden door. It was the entrance to an old abandoned mine shaft and our enterprising restaurateur had the only key. Once inside the shaft, even on the hottest summer days, the temperature would plummet to almost freezing point, so much so, that ice began to form on the outside of the cans which he regularly deposited there.

Sitting one spring day beneath the giant *'Plep l Eger'* tree outside the cafe entrance, I was approached by an old man.

He was wearing part traditional Albanian dress, walked with a stoop and I estimated that he was in his late sixties or early seventies. The old man's hair was snowy white and his chin was peppered with stubble. His

Agron's cold store.

face was wrinkled beyond belief from years of exposure to the elements and when his eyes were closed, he took on the appearance of a corpse. Only his eyes, of the deepest blue, brought his face to life giving a clue to a lifetime of experiences.

The interpreter spoke first. "I think this old gentleman would like to have a word with you. He has something you may be interested in." With that, he proceeded to take out of his coat a crumpled piece of cloth. Inside it was a folded polythene bag. He unwrapped it – carefully.

To our amazement, he was holding a crucifix!

The old man smiled for the first time as he passed it to me. It was about 10 inches high, had the arms missing and was very heavy indeed. I intuitively felt it had to be made of solid silver – I was right.

It was beautiful.

"Where did you get it from?" I asked.

The old man's eyes narrowed. It was obvious his thoughts were taking him back a long way. Twenty five years to be exact, to the day the communists raided his church, stripping it clean of anything of value before setting fire to the structure and burning it to the ground.

The old man had been a devout Roman Catholic as indeed many in that area were and with only minutes' warning of the impending attack, he had gained entry into the church through a side door and rushing to the altar, wrenched the crucifix from its mounting.

The arms were attached to the body by small silver pins and in his haste to save the precious crucifix, the arms remained in place and intact. That night after wrapping the crucifix in cloth and polythene, he buried it close to his home.

That was in 1970.

Enver Hoxha, the tyrannical communist dictator who was in power then and remained so for the next fifteen years until his death in 1985, spent much of his time engaged in the pursuit of 'abolishing God.' It has to be said, he did a pretty good job, depending of course on one's religious affiliation.

Whether or not it had any effect on the old man, I can't say. What I do know is that his desire to part with his 'buried treasure' for the sum of $100 was overwhelming and had increased substantially with every passing day it lay hidden beneath his rows of spring onions.

On the return flight home, the Austrian Airways X-ray machine at Vienna Airport displayed an interesting picture . . .

The officer asked me the question, "Is that what I think it is?" I just nodded. "Enjoy the flight," he added, "I'm sure it'll be a safe one."

To this day, I do not know why I bought the crucifix. Somehow, I felt compelled to, just as I do now to return it. To whom and to where has not yet been decided, but it's just a matter of time – I know.

ostscript:

Tuesday 12th May 1998, the
cifix was returned to Albania. It
s handed over to sister Jose-
ine at the Missionaries of
arity house in Tirana. Two days
er it assumed its rightful place in
Roman Catholic church at
he from whence it came.

Loaded to capacity with emergency Rotary boxes, the convoy winds its

...owards Thethe in the province of Dukagjini.

13

THE NINETEENTH MISSION

Rotary International in Great Britain and Ireland ('RIBI') in a combined operation with 'TFA', had donated three thousand emergency aid boxes during the previous twelve months, to the poorest people in Albania. All consignments were delivered safely to the remote mountain villages of the northern region.

Special thanks go to Eric Harrison, the emergency box scheme co-ordinator from Gatley and District Rotary Club and indeed to all Rotarians nationwide for responding so magnificently. Without doubt, the joint efforts of RIBI in acquiring aid and 'TFA' in transporting and distributing it, ensured that many thousands of Albanians would survive the winter as temperatures plummeted to twenty degrees below freezing.

Eric Harrison (left
a perfect gentleman, her
pictured with the autho

Finding ten roadworthy trucks capable of making the long journey to Dukagjini was difficult to say the least but thanks to the exhaustive efforts of Kole Tonaj, the local member of parliament, it eventually became a reality.

As on previous occasions, the unloading and reloading took place at

Rotary's emergency
box scheme in
operation.

'TFA's safe warehouse in Bajze, which was and is under constant guard by armed police.

Each vehicle had a documented inventory of every Rotary box on board and of course, thanks to some very hard work by Rotarians, the content of each box was itemized, making life for 'TFA's officers in the field a lot easier.

Two trucks went to Thethe and the remaining eight went to the villages of Breglumi, Lotaj, Shoshi, Pulti, Sukaj, Boga, Dedaj and Vuksanaj. Being the first aid ever to arrive in that remote region, the villagers were overwhelmed emotionally and quite overcome with gratitude for the British Rotarians, so far away – who cared.

The remainder of the aid consignment on that occasion consisted of ten pallets of antibiotics, initally donated by Lilley Industries of Basingstoke. Dr. Laurie Ramsey had arranged for past District Governor Brian Thornton of 1040 district to collect them and the President of Castleford Rotary Club, Geoff Hughes, transported them to 'TFA's warehouse in Peterborough.

In total, the antibiotics were worth an estimated £350,000 and would provide enough courses for twenty-eight thousand children.

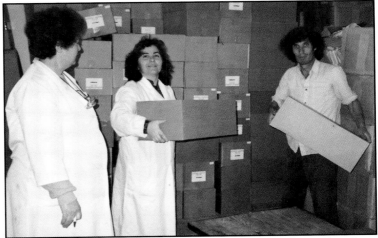

Drugs being safely stored ready for distribution.

Two things were of paramount importance – security and distribution. The Ministry of Health were contacted and were most efficient. A team of officers met us at the docks, arranged customs clearance with almost uncanny speed, provided a guarded warehouse and then distributed the antibiotics with unprecedented haste to every hospital in the country.

I was very fortunate to have two great chaps accompany me on that occasion. Both were making their first trip. Michael Batten who lives at Great Barford, just outside Bedford had been a karate student for fifteen years and held the rank of 3rd Dan Black Belt. At twenty-seven years of age, as well as his obvious physical ability, Michael's caring attitude and sensitivity to people's problems were to be admired.

I first met Kenny Palmer whilst on holiday earlier that year on the island of Lanzarote. I couldn't help being impressed by his sincerity and

The beautiful landscape near Thethe in north eastern Albania.

when the topic of Albania cropped up, he expressed a genuine desire to help and get involved. Kenny earns his living as a professional singer and is an extremely popular entertainer.

Kenny is a compassionate man who nevertheless, always retains his lively sense of humour.

Mr. Pjeter Arbnori was Speaker of the Albanian Parliament, and perhaps the most respected man in the land. He was often described as 'The Mandela of Europe' having spent nearly twenty-nine years in prison being persecuted by the communists. I first saw Pjeter Arbnori in October 1991. He was enjoying his first few days of freedom but he looked very frail after his ordeal. Although I didn't meet him on that occasion, the memory that remained with me for a long time was his absolute sereneness. His face was devoid of any hatred or animosity but I knew nothing at that time of what had happened in the previous twenty-eight years.

In February, 1992, with the communists still in power, 'TFA' had

Michael Batten.

taken twenty juggernauts on our first aid mission to Albania. Conditions were appalling and with eleven trucks unloaded safely in Kavaja, the remaining nine were 'holed up' in Tirana's only 'safe' compound, guarded by the military. Their destination was Shkodra, the northern city where people were starving to death. Using the Tirana Hotel as our headquarters, the thirty man support team were soon joined by twenty irate truck drivers who refused to budge an inch, unless given massive police protection.

To avoid a confrontation, the support team stayed in the background whilst I sat on one side of a large table facing the

"Next time", says Kenny, "shall we tie each pair together?"

twenty truck drivers on the other. Suddenly, a man sat down next to me with an interpreter – it was Pjeter Arbnori, he had heard of my plight and driven fifty miles from Shkodra. Four hours later, the situation was finally resolved, the trucks completed their journey and one hundred and eighty tonnes of vital food got through. I had Pjeter to thank for that.

His concern for my safety and well being during that four hour 'discussion' was paramount. He

Pjeter Arbnori, often described as 'The Mandela of Europe' after having spent twenty-eight and a half years in prison being persecuted by the Communists, is today speaker of the Albanian Parliament and perhaps the most respected man in the land.

131

saw the pain in my eyes and desperately sought to reduce the tension.

Six months later I learned of his story from Bill Hamilton, who had completed an in depth interview for his book *Albania Who Cares*. Shortly afterwards, I met Pjeter for the second time and he was so incredibly apologetic for the problems I had experienced that day at the Tirana Hotel.

There is little doubt he has suffered more than most men alive enduring the horrors of Burrel Prison at the hands of the 'Sigurimi' (secret police). Why? Because he dared to speak out against communism.

There can be absolutely no earthly comparison between my four hour argument and his *twenty-eight and a half years torture*, but to him, the most compassionate of men, a powerful empathy existed.

It was our first visit to Tirana's maternity hospital and nothing could have prepared us for what we were about to see. We knew about incubators, but we always thought each baby should have its own! Instead, there were sometimes two or three babies in each!

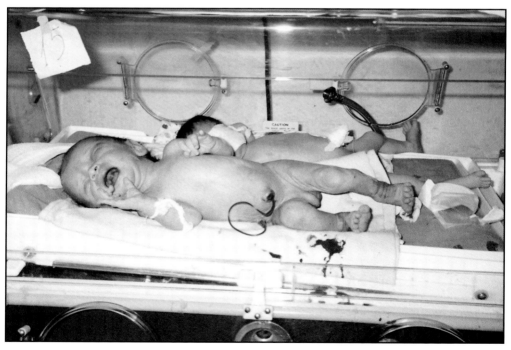

The babies we had to help.

When we met the hospital's director Dr. Zhani Treska and the Chief of Neonatology Dr. Eduart Tushe, their faces matched their handshakes. The despair was obvious. "It's very difficult for me," said Dr. Treska, "to admit women into hospital to give birth prematurely for their own safety, when their babies have no hope of survival in the absence of an infant ventilator. We need at least three here in Tirana and we haven't got a single one."

The Oximeter-Criticare 504 we had brought was small consolation but gave renewed hope to an otherwise dispirited group of medics. Costing 'TFA' £1,500, Charles Hutton of The New Victoria Hospital in Kingston-upon-Thames contributed £500.

Looking around the wards, the overwhelming necessity was for infant ventilators. Transportation to Albania was not a problem, but at £6,500 each, cost certainly was.

Postscript – (1st January 1998)

Altogether, members of 'TFA' visited the safe warehouse in Bajze on ten separate occasions, where it served admirably in protecting both the aid and the team from attack. It had been arranged especially for us by Dode Kacaj, the local MP and was in actual fact a redundant railway station and siding. A few miles north, the line crossed the border into Montenegro but no trains had run since the present troubles began in 1991.

Time and time again we were reassured by everyone that this railway station was the *'safest place in the whole of northern Albania'*. There were electronic gates, a high perimeter wall and security in the form of a twenty-four hour police patrol. It couldn't be better. On numerous occasions we asked the question, "What is there here to guard?" There were only a few empty sheds and twenty or so deserted railway carriages.

Most people remember where they were when John F. Kennedy died, or what they were doing when they heard of the crash which killed Princess Diana. I was tucking into a large 'koran', Albania's most succulent fish when I learned the truth about Bajze's now infamous railway station. I suddenly lost my appetite.

Amongst the derelict railway carriages were five containers of radioactive waste! We were absolutely stunned.

When Germany decided to rid itself of a large consignment of this waste, it looked around for an ideal dumping ground to deposit it. Somewhere within its own borders was politically and morally unacceptable and in looking further afield, what better place could there be than Europe's poorest country – Albania.

Getting it in, using unmarked containers by rail through Titograd was the perfect answer. Depositing it just a few miles inside the Albanian border at Bajze station was an ingenious plan.

Three million Albanians, had they known, may have disagreed. The fact was, they knew nothing of this nocturnal German 'sortie.' The secret was shared only by some ruthless politicians lining their grubby little pockets at their people's expense.

With the passage of time, EU legislation was passed in Brussels preventing such appalling acts taking place ever again. Germany was reprimanded and ordered to take back its radio-active waste, which it did and very quickly too.

Just what happens to the children of Bajze in twenty years time is anyone's guess and should their worst fear come true, the German Government will have one more atrocity to answer for, but by then – it will be too late!

For those who went only to help, with no ulterior motive whatsoever, the irony may be more poignant that we ever imagined.

An Albanian policeman having a 'bit of fun.' Perhaps he would have wiped the smile off his face if he had known of the contents of the five railway carriages in front of him.

Obituary – May 1998

The funeral took place on 3rd May of Dode Kacaj, Member of Parliament for Malsia e Madhe. A simple ceremony was held in his home town of Bajze. Dode was fifty-one years old and died of *cancer*. He is survived by his wife Vlora and his two teenage sons Aren and Johan.

...ring 1992 and this lone tree in the mountains near Vlora could almost
...e been signalling a new beginning for Albania. A week earlier, the
...nocratic landslide had put the country in jubilant mood.

14
'PITKINI'

Andre Axford of the ACO Organisation, a group responsible for business relations between Albania and the United Kingdom, telephoned me in late November 1994 with an invitation to accompany him on a promotional trip in January 1995. He was in the process of inviting several other British charities but most importantly had also invited that wonderful comedian and film star, Mr. Norman Wisdom.

The trip would commence 19th January and would cover four days. An intensive schedule was being prepared which would involve official functions, cultural evenings, a charity day and low key promotion for British business in Albania.

The reader could be forgiven for asking the question "Why Norman Wisdom?" The answer is quite simple. During the long years of the Hoxha regime, when most laws were at the mercy of his every whim (in his infinite wisdom he even abolished 'God'), Enver Hoxha, try as he might, could find no western propaganda material whatsoever in the films and activities of Mr. Norman Pitkin, Norman Wisdom's hard done by little character.

Consequently, night after night, Hoxha decreed that Norman Wisdom films should be screened – and they were.

As a result of this constant exposure Norman became very well known and liked by virtually every Albanian family. Perhaps there was something in the Albanian psyche they could relate to or identify with. Whatever, most Albanians felt Norman was a member of their own family and loved him dearly.

Without doubt 'Pitkini' as he is known, is the biggest star in Albania. He had never previously visited the country but always wanted to and when the people knew he was coming, pandemonium broke out.

Just days away from his eightieth birthday, Norman was the life and soul of the party. He was very fit and had the most amazing vitality. As the reader will see from the following programme, Norman was 'on the go' most of the time. He was a great ambassador for Britain and the Albanian people loved him. None more so than the children. They all cried with *laughter* while he was there and cried *tears of sorrow* when he left.

As Stephen Nash, the British chargé d'affaires remarked – "Albania will never be the same again".

*orman listens intently at a celebration dinner to welcome him to
irana, in an address by the British chargé d'affaires Mr. Stephen Nash.*

NORMAN 'PITKINI' WISDOM
VISIT TO TIRANA, ALBANIA
19th-22nd January 1995

PROGRAMME
Thursday 19th January 1995
06.00 Check in at Heathrow Airport, Terminal Two
06.45 Reception by Austrian Airlines in VIP lounge
07.35 Depart Heathrow
10.35 Arrive Vienna
12.05 Depart Vienna
14.05 Arrive Tirana
14.15 Welcome reception by Mayor of Tirana, British chargé d'affaires
14.45 Depart Airport for accommodation in Tirana
18.00 Variety performance by the Academy of Fine Arts
20.30 Dinner hosted by Sali Kelmendi, Mayor of Tirana

Norman with the author.

Friday 20th January 1995
09.00 Visit Feed the Children Aid project - No. 1 Hospital, Tirana
09.30 Visit Task Force Albania project - No. 1 Hospital, Tirana
10.00 Visit Blood Transfusion project - No. 1 Hospital, Tirana
11.00 Visit ADRA project - Official Opening of the 'Pitkin Centre'
12.00 Lunch
14.00 Audience with H E President Dr. Sali Berisha
15.30 Visit Childhope Street Children's Hostel
16.30 Visit Red Cross Centre
20.00 Dinner hosted by Stephen Nash, British chargé d'affaires

Here, Norman breaks all the rules of protocol and President Berisha was delighted.

Saturday 21st January 1995
10.00 Presentation of 'Freedom of the City' at Academy of Fine Arts
10.30 Thirty minute comedy show by the Academy of Fine Arts
11.30 Walk-about from University Square to Skenderbeg Square
13.00 Lunch
15.00 Visit the Children's Hospital in Tirana
16.30 Dystrophic Hospital
20.00 Variety show on live TVSH
21.00 Interview and talk show on live TVSH

Three thousand children pack The Palace of Sports to see 'Pitkini.'

Sunday 22nd January 1995
10.00. Palace of Sports, three thousand children/teenagers talk and
autographs
13.00 Leave Tirana for airport
15.00 Depart Tirana
17.00 Arrive Vienna
18.45 Depart Vienna
20.15 Arrive Heathrow, Terminal Two

*Tired and exhausted (except for Norman who was as fresh as
a daisy) the team arrive back at Heathrow.*

15
THE TWENTY-FIRST MISSION

In January 1995, the speaker of the Albanian Parliament, Mr. Pjeter Arbnori contacted Task Force Albania through his assistant and interpreter Mrs. Enjellushe Shquarri.

I first met 'Angela' in 1993 when she accompanied a group of parliamentarians to London, acting as their official translator. Why she had been given the job was obvious. A woman of excellent integrity, gentle, feminine and last but not least, most efficient. Indeed, in the previous two years, whenever preliminary negotiations began with particular MPs representing areas we planned to send humanitarian aid to, it was Angela who did all the ground work, without which, 'TFA' would have had major problems.

"I have a favour to ask you John, is it possible you could take aid to the town of Librazsd?" she continued. "The people of that area are so poor – they have nothing." I knew that if Angela was asking, it was necessary and without further ado, told her to contact the local deputeti (MP)

On 26th March, a thirty-eight tonne truck left 'TFA's Peterborough warehouse. On board were four consignments. The first consisted of five hundred English books, patiently collected by children from the Kingston-upon-Thames area in Surrey, all members of the Beavers, Cub Scouts, Scouts, Brownies and Girl Guides. The lucky recipients were pupils at a school in Tirana and their delight defied imagination.

The second consisted of sixteen timber medical cabinets each containing highly sophisticated medical apparatus. It meant very little to us but in Dr. Afrim Tabaku from Tirana University it produced a totally different response. Thirdly, were thirty boxes of assorted clothing destined for Shkodra's 'Tefik G'yli' orphanage.

Last but not least the main thrust of the mission was to deliver nine hundred and twenty boxes of clothing and bedding to Librazsd and the surrounding villages.

Angela had contacted the Deputeti for Librazsd, a Mr. Pëllumb Malaj, and informed him of our arrival time and cargo. From the outset his organisation was most impressive. He met us at Rinas airport, took care of all customs requirements for the aid and arranged a substantial police escort to an army compound in Tirana where he provided four military trucks to transfer the consignments to Librazsd.

So happy — this ten year old mountain girl holding on tight to her 'first real pair of shoes'.

'Christmas in April.'

Not taking any chances whatsoever, the trucks overnighted at the police headquarters and the following morning set out for the remote villages high in the snow-covered surrounding mountains.

The first destination was the commune of Sterbleve and the distribution of aid to the villages of Llanga, with one hundred and seven families, Zobrun with one hundred and thirty-seven families and Borov with one hundred and forty-seven. Finally we reached Sterbleve itself and the two hundred and nine families who lived there.

In all the years we have been taking aid to Albania, we have never seen people so destitute or so relieved. Most had never seen a foreigner before and when we arrived at our second destination, the commune of Qender with aid for the two hundred and sixty families of Bobje and the sixty of Arres, we found conditions even worse.

Distribution was administered by seven senior officials of the ruling council, Hasan Ballgjini, Naun Sinani, Mitab Tole, Pëllumb Gjini, Nazif Kurti, Dilaver Teta and Fatmir Venetkiu. In all, nine hundred and twenty boxes were shared amongst nine hundred and twenty families and we had barely scratched the surface. Later we found out that in Pëllumb Malaj's constituency there were sixty villages with many worse than we had seen. What was needed was a reappraisal of our work in Albania and the possibility of including a massive and concentrated emergency aid scheme to this impoverished area.

An ambitious plan got under way to clothe the entire zone of Librazsd. With one hundred and thirty-eight thousand people facing the bleakest of futures, 'TFA' had only got until the end of September before the snows came when most of the villages would be cut off.

A massive campaign was launched to collect ten thousand boxes of both children's and adults' clothes and shoes. It would take ten juggernaut trucks to transport them to Albania and an application was made to the Overseas Development Administration (ODA) for funding.

oments of great happiness
— captured for posterity

Right:
He didn't know – or
care – that it was a
lady's fur coat.

Left:
By chance we came across a gypsy
encampment and Elaine, seen here
comforting a little baby whose mother
was very ill, dressed the child in a
new knitted jumper courtesy of the
English ladies' group 'Inner Wheel.'

Right:
Interpreter Andi Zhugli,
Sue Cowley and Elaine
Seabrook pose for this
picture with the matron
and staff of the Teufik
G'yli orphanage.

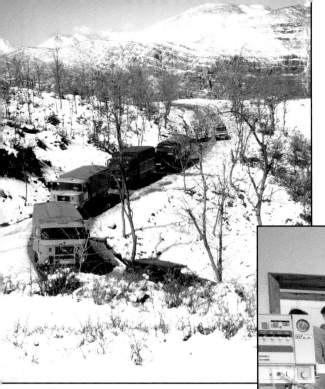

ve:

*e Republican Guard' helping us
ch mountain villages.*

ow:

*'s Elaine Seabrook bringing a
moments of happiness to
na,' a little orphan girl.*

The paediatric ventilator in action.

147

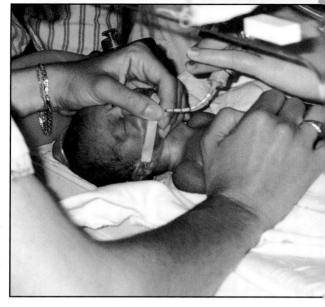

The ventilator arrives 'in the nick of time' as this baby changed colour from pink to lilac – to purple and then black.

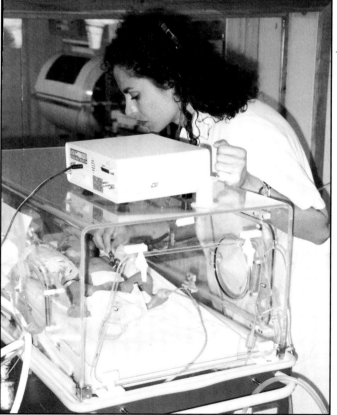

Thanks to the ventilator and some precision heart massage by Dr. Linda Ciu, the baby was saved.

Author's note: When we delivered the ventilator, we did not expect to witness a real life-saving situation. From the moment the alarm sounded, Dr. Ciu took control. She didn't speak but had an amazing calming influence on the whole team. Ten minutes later all the nurses and doctors smiled and breathed a sigh of relief.

Cowley discovers being an aid worker brings special rewards. Here befriends little 'Mimoza', an orphan suffering with severe eye problems.

'Lollypops'

An old Albanian lady pictured here on a mountainside road near Elbasan.

Right:
Tirana Maternity Hospital had no infant ventilators whatsoever. That meant, if a woman gave birth to a baby prematurely, certainly before its lungs were properly formed – it would die! 'TFA' very proudly delivered an infant ventilator costing twenty thousand dollars which immediately saved a girl's life. Here the author hands it over officially to the chief of neonatology Dr. Eduart Tushe.

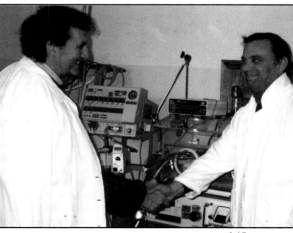

'Mimoza' the orphaned girl from Shkodra.

16
THE TWENTY-THIRD MISSION

ometime in May 1995, at the suggestion of Eric Harrison, Rotary International's emergency box scheme co-ordinator, I telephoned Mrs. Doce Kruger. It was my first contact with The Association of Inner Wheel Clubs in Gt. Britain and Ireland and Doce was the chairman of the Association's Overseas Service Committee. The fifty-five thousand members of Inner Wheel are all wives of Rotarians. They support the one thousand one hundred clubs nationwide.

A leaflet was circulated to all branches in June and the response from club members was quite incredible. By August, two thousand family boxes had been donated and delivered to 'TFA's warehouse at No. 1 hangar, RAF Cardington in Bedfordshire.

This combined operation between 'TFA' and the Inner Wheel Clubs proved extremely successful and on 28th September high up in the remote mountains of central eastern Albania, all two thousand boxes were handed over to the head of each family in the village of Barbe near Librazd.

The villagers were so grateful as they had never received any aid before and were quite the poorest people we had ever seen. Indeed, many of the children had no shoes, a frightening thought considering the harsh Balkan winter was only days away. With fifty-nine other villages spread over one hundred square miles of remote mountain terrain, 'TFA' had an enormous task ahead over the following two years. Had it not been for the concern and assistance of Inner Wheel's President Mrs. Vivienne Bolton together with the club Overseas Service Organisers, the villagers of Barbe would have been faced with a very, very grim winter!

Ten thousand family boxes were transported on this trip, many of them coming from schoolchildren in Bedfordshire, Cambridgeshire and Hertfordshire, together with support from the WI in those counties.

There is little doubt that this mission was one of our most succesful. In one effort, ten thousand families each received a large box of warm winter clothing and bedding. Their happiness was indescribable and the looks on their faces will remain with me always.

Everywhere, I saw hundreds of beautiful children, most of whom will probably never have the chance to realise their full potential. I was reminded of the lines from Gray's Elegy:

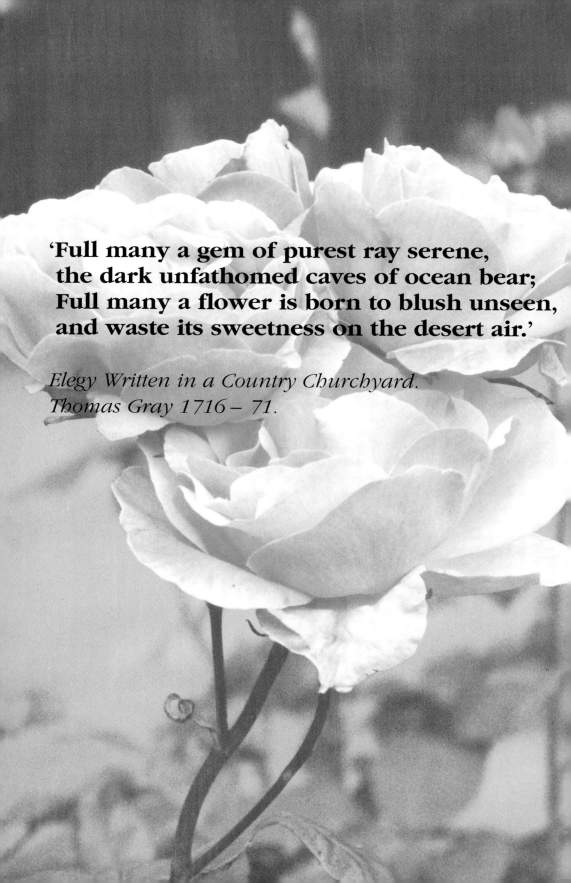

'Full many a gem of purest ray serene,
the dark unfathomed caves of ocean bear;
Full many a flower is born to blush unseen,
and waste its sweetness on the desert air.'

Elegy Written in a Country Churchyard.
Thomas Gray 1716 – 71.

Eyrl.

Veteran aid worker Alan Blake doing what he does so well.

Shpresa Vreto, secretary of the voluntary children's association 'The Little Mermaid' receiving a four wheel drive Toyota car from 'TFA's director. The vehicle will enable material to be delivered monthly to thousands of deprived children in remote areas.

153

Exhausted cameraman Tim Eyrl managing a smile.

In her element. Irene Leslie, 'TFA's Honorary Secretary from Dunstable at the orphanage.

The Albanian Republican Guard assist with the unloading of the trucks

'TFA's Alan Bristow being mobbed by mountain children after seeing sweets for the first time.

The support team.

Darren Gill of Bedford giving out the aid.

A mother prepares dinner for her family in the only way she knows how.

In an interview with John van Weenen, the President of Albania, Dr. Sali Berisha, expresses his gratitude to the ladies of the British Inner Wheel Association.

A SMILE

A SMILE COSTS NOTHING,
but gives much. It enriches those
who receive, without making poorer
those who give. It takes but a moment, but
the memory of it sometimes lasts forever.
None is so rich or mighty that he can
get along without it, and none is so poor
but that he can be made rich by it.
A smile creates happiness in the home,
fosters goodwill in business, and is the
countersign of friendship. It brings
rest to the weary, cheer to the discouraged,
sunshine to the sad, and it is Nature's
best antidote for trouble. Yet it cannot
be bought, begged, borrowed or stolen,
for it is something that is of no value
to anyone until it is given away.
Some people are too tired to give you a
smile, give them one of yours, as none
needs a smile so much as he who has
no more to give.

Anon.

17
MOTHER TERESA
1910-1997

In June 1992, President Berisha bestowed upon John the nation's highest civilian honour, 'The Order of Mother Teresa.' He very proudly accepted it, on behalf of all those who had assisted him, from Albania's most famous citizen herself.

159

In February 1993, I had a unique opportunity to visit Calcutta to meet Albania's most famous citizen – Mother Teresa. No words could adequately express my admiration and respect for the tiny, frail eighty-five year old lady who arrived in 1937 in Entally, a suburb of Calcutta, with just a five rupee note – and a lot of faith. Never once asking for government backing or church funding, she managed to build a vast network of Missionaries of Charity worldwide. To the world's destitute, she gave hope. To the poor, afflicted and diseased she showed love. In the troubled times in which we live, she restored faith in human nature and for years she had been thought of by many as *a living saint*.

May 1994 and John meets Mother Teresa in London and gives her the good news that British Airways have agreed to give her and her companion free air travel, to any part of the world, for the rest of her life.

Talking to her in April 1993, having just returned from the Great Highlands after delivering medical aid, with the invaluable help of Alan Bristow, Azad Kumar and Alan Blake, I had noticed she was troubled.

A major problem for her, her organisation having grown so large, was getting from country to country. She had to rely on charity and as she never asked for it – it wasn't always forthcoming.

"Perhaps," I said, "I should have a word with British Airways on my return to London." "Would you really?" she replied. "That would be wonderful." I have to say, not knowing anyone at BA and starting from

"*I am nothing; I am but an instrument, a tiny pencil in the hands of the Lord with which he writes what he likes. However imperfect we are, he writes beautifully*".
M. Teresa M.C.

LDM.   9-9-93

Dear Mr. John van Weenen

Thank you for sending the letter of Mr. Gary Gray.

Thank you also for getting me the Assistance for my travelling.

God has been very good to me a number of Air Lines have given me the help. So I have much to thank God for.

My gratitude to you is my prayer for you and your family

God bless you
M Teresa mc

REPUBLIKA E SHQIPERISE

PRESIDENTI I REPUBLIKES

I JEP

JOHN VAN WEENEN

Urdhrin
"NENE TEREZA"

Tiranë më, 30.5.1992
Dekret Nr: 197

PRESIDENTI
SALI BERISHA

PER VEPRIMTARI HUMANE DHE FISNIKE
NE NDIHME TE SHQIPERISE DHE PER NDJENJAT
MIQESORE HUMANITARE E BAMIRESE NDAJ POPU-
LLIT SHQIPTAR.

URDHRI
"NENE TEREZA"

The order of Mother Teresa

scratch, was a shade daunting but I was determined to help this lady at all costs.

A week later, from executive level came the answer I had been hoping for. British Airways would provide Mother Teresa and her travelling companion with free first class tickets, to travel at will on any British Airways route, anywhere in the world, for the rest of her life. I thought to myself, 'Mother will be pleased'.

 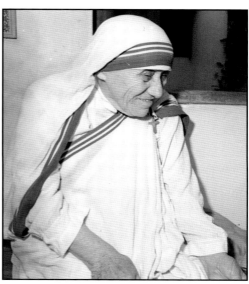

Master Gichin Funakoshi   **_Mother Teresa_**

Recently, whilst reading Funakoshi Sensei's _Karate-dō Kyōhan_, considered by many as the bible of karate, I came to the chapter entitled 'Maxims for the Trainee'. Although I had read this piece many times before, a couple of lines seemed to take on a whole new meaning.

'Make benevolence your lifelong duty. This surely is an important mission. It is a lifelong effort, truly a long journey.'

How strange I thought. In one sentence he had encapsulated the whole meaning of 'Karate-dō' whilst epitomising the long struggle and unselfish dedication of a certain, rather special Loreto nun.

On Friday 5th September 1997, the world learned that Mother Teresa of Calcutta had died of a heart attack. Thousands upon thousands filed past her body to pay their last respects as it lay in state at St. Thomas's Church. The Nobel Laureate's body had been taken from 'Mother House,' the headquarters of the Missionaries of Charity she founded to look after the dying, the destitute and the unwanted.

Her head and body were draped in the distinctive blue-bordered white cotton sari, the uniform of her order, surrounded by white lotus flowers and roses.

As the mourners streamed by, each was given a rose by a nun who told them 'it's from Mother'.

Such was the standing of Mother Teresa, that Saturday 13th September, the day of her funeral was declared a national day of mourning. On that day, her body was draped in the Indian flag and carried on the gun carriage that bore the bodies of Mahatma Gandhi and Jawaharlal Nehru.

The six hour funeral ceremony was conducted by Cardinal Angelo Sodano, the Vatican's Secretary of State and the Pope's special representative. After the mass, Sister Nirmala, Mother Teresa's successor, pledged that her work would go on, undiminished by her passing. The future of the order, with five hundred and eighty-four houses in one hundred and fifteen countries is now in the hands of sixty-three year old Sister Nirmala, ironically, a Hindu convert.

When questioned by journalists about the future of the Missionaries of Charity, all she would say was "God will provide whatever we need." Her blind faith and her inheritance of Mother Teresa's most devastating weapon, that of *'innocent sincerity'* when responding to critical questions, may well be enough – time will tell.

On Saturday 6th September, the day after Mother Teresa passed away, I met Sister Theresina at Westminster Abbey. *The very sad occasion was the funeral of Diana, Princess of Wales* and when I offered my condolences to Sister Theresina who is the head sister for the UK and Ireland, she said "Don't be upset, Mother is in heaven now – she is with God".

I thought about that – how wonderful for her.

What an incredible difference this one lady has made to the world. Without doubt Albania's most famous daughter – born on 26th August 1910 in the town of Skopje, now in Macedonia. Christened 'Agnes Bojaxhiu', she was nicknamed 'Gonxha' meaning 'flower bud' in Albanian and the desire to become a nun first surfaced when she was only twelve years of age. In the years that followed, her relationship with Father Jambren Kovic was to have a far reaching effect on Agnes, especially when years later, she entered the Entally convent in Calcutta.

As Mother put it, "At eighteen I decided to leave home and become a nun. By then I realised my vocation was towards the poor. From then on, I have never had the least doubt of my decision." Pointing a finger towards heaven, she added – *"He made the choice."*

In joining the Loreto Order, her route to Bengal was by way of Rathfarnham in Ireland where she spent two months as a young postulant and in November 1928, set sail for India – and Calcutta.

So her life began as a novice, and in March 1931, she took her first vows of poverty, chastity and obedience as a Sister of Loreto. She also felt inspired to take her name in religious form from a French nun called Thérèse Martin, who in 1927 was canonised by the Vatican with the title,

'St. Thérèse of Lisieux'.

Her noviciate completed, Sister Teresa as she was now called, was sent to teach at St. Mary's School, a part of Loreto Convent in the Calcutta suburb of Entally. She was to remain there for seventeen happy years. It was during that time she met Father Celeste van Exem, a man who would have an enormous influence on her life.

Sister Teresa took her final vows on 24th May 1939 and returned to St. Mary's convent where she became 'Superior' and known by all as 'Mother Teresa'.

During the war years, Mother Teresa worked tirelessly with the poor and afflicted as she had done in the years prior and on 10th September 1946, received *an inner command* to go and serve the poor in the streets. "The message was clear," she said – *"it was an order."*

"I was to leave the convent. I felt God wanted something more from me. He wanted me to be poor and to love him in the distressing disguise of the poorest of poor."

Mother Teresa knew she had to leave the Loreto Order, yet remain a nun. The monumental task of convincing Rome it was in everyone's best interest, especially hers, was complicated, protracted and without precedent.

Two years later on 8th August 1948, Father van Exem was permitted by the Archbishop to break the good news to Mother Teresa. On hearing it, her first question was, "Father, can I go to the slums now?" On 17th August, Mother Teresa wore her distinctive white sari with the blue border for the very first time.

The following year her work took her to the slums of Motijhil, a huge undertaking involving new schools, hospitals and looking after the poorest of the poor where tetanus, cholera, meningitis and plague were commonplace.

In February 1953, the Missionary of Charity sisters moved into Lower Circular Road, Calcutta. The property was to become the Order's headquarters and soon become known as 'Motherhouse.'

The first two homes outside Calcutta were opened in 1960 in Ranchi and Delhi, the latter by Prime Minister Nehru himself. Soon Mother's Houses sprang up everywhere in virtually every town and city in the land.

It was inevitable that Mother Teresa would carry her work overseas, and in 1965, her first non Indian house was opened in Cocorote in Venezuela. Thirty-three years later, five hundred and eighty-four houses exist in one hundred and fifteen countries!

The author is grateful for relevant information and the following extract from Navin Chawla's superb biography – 'Mother Teresa.'

Mother Teresa's name invariably conjured up a vision of a small, frail woman in a white sari, offering love and compassion to the poorest of the poor who live in the slums of Calcutta, in cardboard boxes in London, in the ghettos of New York, and in the shadow of the Vatican itself.

In recognition of her unique work, the world lavished on her its highest honours and awards, from the Nobel Peace Prize to the Order of Merit presented by Queen Elizabeth. These she accepted only in the name of the poor, whom she and her Missionaries of Charity served so devotedly.

"I am but a pencil in the hands of the Lord, it is his work," she repeatedly said.

Mother Teresa will be greatly missed – by the world, but I am reminded of Sister Theresina's words of comfort: *"Don't be upset, Mother is in heaven, now – she is with God."*

The entrance to 'Motherhouse' at 54A Lower Circular Road, Calcutta. A small board announced whether Mother Teresa was 'in' or 'out'.

A Simple Prayer

Lord make me an instrument
of thy peace...
where there is hatred,
let me sow love;
where there is injury, pardon;
where there is doubt, faith;
where there is despair, hope;
where there is darkness, light;
where there is sadness, joy;
O Divine Master,
grant that I may not
so much seek to be consoled
as to console;
to be understood
as to understand;
to be loved as to love;
for it is in giving
that we receive;
it is in pardoning
that we are pardoned;
and it is in dying
that we are born
to eternal life.

St Francis of Assisi

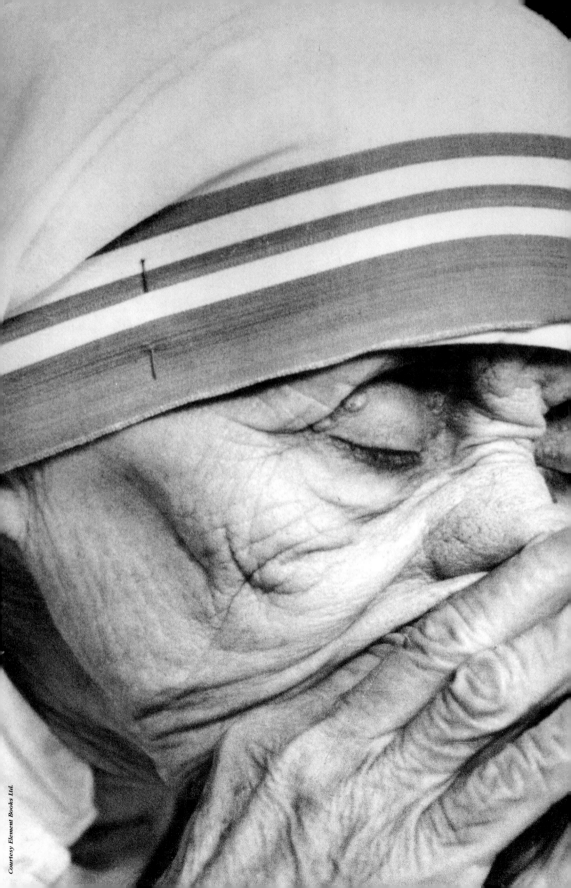

Mother Teresa

"It will be for posterity to decide if she is a saint.

I can only say that in a dark time she is a burning and

shining light;

in a carnal time, a living embodiment of

Christ's gospel of love; in a godless time,

the Word dwelling amongst us, full of grace and truth."

Malcolm Muggeridge
'Something Beautiful For God'
Harper Collins Publishers

Desmond Cooper of Willington in Bedfordshire was quite adamant should have the small pink card, he held in his hand, one spring day in 1994. The words written on it, reproduced opposite, immediately struck a cord. Not **'taking time'** for the important things in life, had for me, regrettably been a reality. I dropped the card inside my Albanian address book for safe keeping.

Months later, in Albania, I had gone to meet aid trucks at Durres dock. Three of Mother Teresa's nuns were there also, meeting sisters from Italy and whilst we were talking, the card, for some strange reason, fell out of n address book.

The tallest sister picked it up, noticed the title, and asked if she may re it. "With pleasure," I said. As she neared the end, I saw the tears welling in her eyes. Unconsciously, I turned my head away. The words had touche her. "May I write them down," she asked. I just nodded.

Five minutes later, she completed the last line. "They are beautiful," she said, "I will give them to every sister in Albania – thank you." With that, three sisters turned and walked in the direction of the ferry that had just berthed.

I stood there, alone, watching but not wanting them to go. Suddenly, t sister who had written down the words stopped. She lifted her head a littl and turned to face me, her eyes caught mine for just a moment – "God bless you," she said. I wanted to reply but was unsure how to.

As they walked further away, a large truck drove between us. It seemed an eternity till it had passed. I looked for the sisters but only the empty dockyard stared back at me. They had gone.

I never saw them again.

Two years later, whilst visiting the Missionaries of Charity house in Shkodra, I noticed a young sister take a small card from a fold in her 'sari. Sitting down in a corner, quietly she began to read the words on the card.

The courtyard was teaming with activity and no one was aware of the young sister nor the beautiful smile on her face. As she finished reading, sl looked up, our eyes met.

"I know John you're leaving for Tirana," she said, "and are anxious to b there before nightfall, but could you spare a moment to share these words with me? – I know you'll like them."

I sat down on the ground next to her, "Yes," I replied – **"I have all the time in the world."**

TAKE TIME

"Take time to think,
it is the source of power.

Take time to play,
it is the secret of perpetual youth.

Take time to read,
it is the fountain of wisdom.

Take time to pray,
it is the greatest power on earth.

Take time to love and be loved,
it is a God given privilege.

Take time to be friendly,
it is the road to happiness.

Take time to laugh,
it is the music of the soul.

Take time to give,
it is too short a day to be selfish.

Take time to work,
it is the price of success.

Take time to do charity,
it is the key to heaven."

Pope John Paul II greets Mother Teresa in Albania in April 1995.

18
POPE JOHN PAUL II

I n late February 1993, the Vatican made an unusual announcement. Pope John Paul II would be visiting Albania. So what was unusual about that? Tirana wasn't a million miles from Rome, a mere thirty minutes by air.

True, but the last time a reigning Pontiff set foot on Albanian soil was over four hundred years ago. It was a very special occasion.

Arriving at Rinas airport, His Holiness was transported by road to a rendezvous just south of the city of Shkodra, where he was met by local dignitaries. After several speeches and a short ceremony, the Pope boarded the 'Popemobile' and was driven to the cathedral in Shkodra.

During the Hoxha years, this fine cathedral building had been turned into a 'basketball stadium' but with the dictator's death in 1985, it was hastily converted back into a 'House of God' for all Roman Catholics in northern Albania.

The crowd await the arrival of the Pope at Shkodra Cathedral.

The Member of Parliament for Dukagjini had been with us in the preceeding week, whilst delivering aid to Malsia e Madhe, and he arranged for Alan Bristow and myself to attend the ceremony that afternoon in Shkodra Cathedral.

Crowds lined the city streets as the 'Popemobile' slowly made its way along the route.

The reason behind the Pope's visit was the ordination of three Archbishops and many of the top clergy from many European countries had made the pilgrimage to be there for this historic occasion. Mother Teresa, who had not been in Albania for some time, had co-ordinated her trip with that of the Pontiff and took her place in the congregation along with other sisters from her Shkodra house. The atmosphere was buzzing with anticipation. Government officials and ministers filled the front pews whilst the choir, specially flown in for the occasion from neighbouring Kosovo, took its place.

Pope John Paul II appears on the balcony at Shkodra Cathedral in November 1993 with the three newly-ordained Archbishops.

The service was beautiful, and afterwards, in brilliant spring sunshine the Pope appeared before the crowd on the balcony of the adjoining building. His message was for peace, stability and happiness and he asked all gathered there that day to pray for peace in the former Yugoslavia.

As he left the cathedral, crowds lined the streets once more, just to catch a glimpse of him before he disappeared into a helicopter. Lifting off, it headed for Tirana and the one hundred thousand people who had filled Skanderbeg Square to hear his goodwill message.

All went well, and at 7.00 p.m. that April evening, Pope John Paul II's aeroplane left the concrete runway at Rinas airport and disappeared westwards into the sunset, leaving behind a nation wondering whether a Pope really had visited their country, after a period of four hundred years, or had it just been a dream after all!

19
THE PRINCESS OF WALES 1961-1997

"Nothing brings me more happiness than trying to help the most vulnerable people in society. It is a goal and an essential part of my life, a kind of destiny. Whoever is in distress can call on me. I will come running, wherever they are."
Diana, Princess of Wales, June 1997.

In October 1996, I received a telephone call from a very good friend of mine, Jed Fortune-Ford, the well known entertainer. He offered to fund-raise for 'TFA' and in his inimitable style, began writing to hundreds of Midlands-based companies, with, I might say, surprising results.

On 18th November 1996, I asked Jed if he would pen a letter to Princess Diana, enclosing a video of 'TFA's work, and inviting her to join us on a future trip and see first hand the appalling conditions that still prevailed in many children's orphanages.

In all honesty – I didn't expect a reply.

How wrong I was. Two days later we received a telephone call from Victoria Mendem, who at that time, was Princess Diana's Personal Assistant. "The Princess of Wales has asked me to telephone you immediately. Last night, she watched your video in its entirety and was extremely upset at what she saw. Yes, she will go to Albania with you – she thanks you for your kind invitation and wonders how she can help in the meantime."

Sadly, the political situation in Albania was deteriorating fast. Within weeks the pyramid savings schemes would collapse bringing chaos and anarchy. (See Chapter 30, 'The Political Quagmire').

Princess Diana's safety was our primary concern, so quite rightly, her visit was put on the 'back burner'. She insisted on being 'kept posted' of all developments and on 3rd January 1997, a letter arrived from St. James's Palace via her new PA Jacqueline Allen containing a cheque for five hundred pounds.

We were both flattered and honoured.

In June 1997, elections brought the socialists to power and by August 1997, normality was returning to the country. Hopes within 'TFA' were high for a visit by the Princess in 1998 and accordingly, whilst in Tirana

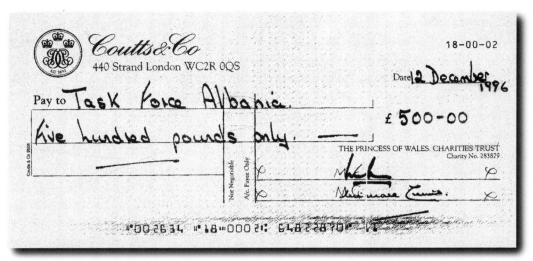

on 14th August 1997, I began making discreet enquiries. A little over two weeks later I returned, full of optimism and very excited, to be greeted by the most horrendous news…

The rest is history.

On returning home from work at 10.30 p.m. on Wednesday 3rd September, there were two messages on the answer machine. Both were from the Lord Chamberlain's office at Buckingham Palace. Ten invitations to Task Force Albania had been allocated for the memorial service at Westminster Abbey.

No words can describe the feelings the service evoked. It was so sad.

In honour of that remarkable young woman, I include the full text of the funeral service of Diana – Princess of Wales.

ORDER OF SERVICE

The Cortège preceded by the Collegiate Body, moves to the Quire and Sacrarium, during which the Choir sings

THE SENTENCES

I AM the resurrection and the life, saith the Lord: he that believeth in me, though he were dead, yet shall he live: and whosoever liveth and believeth in me shall never die.

St John 11: 25, 26

I KNOW that my Redeemer liveth, and that he shall stand at the latter day upon the earth: and though after my skin worms destroy this body, yet in my flesh shall I see God: whom I shall see for myself, and mine eyes shall behold, and not another.

Job 19: 25-27

WE brought nothing into this world, and it is certain we can carry nothing out.

1 Timothy 6: 7

The Lord gave, and the Lord hath taken away; blessed be the name of the Lord.

William Croft (1678 - 1727)
Organist of Westminster abbey 1708-27

Job 1: 21

THOU knowest, Lord, the secrets of our hearts; shut not thy merciful ears unto our prayer; but spare us, Lord most holy, O God most mighty, O holy and most merciful Saviour, thou most worthy Judge eternal, suffer us not, at our last hour, for any pains of death, to fall from thee. Amen.

Book of Common Prayer

Henry Purcell (1659-95)
Organist of Westminster Abbey 1679-95

I HEARD a voice from heaven, saying unto me Write, From henceforth blessed are the dead which die in the Lord: even so saith the Spirit; for they rest from their labours.

Revelation 14: 13

William Croft

All remain standing. The Very Reverend Dr. Wesley Carr, Dean of Westminster, says

THE BIDDING

WE are gathered here in Westminster Abbey to give thanks for the life of Diana, Princess of Wales; to commend her soul to almighty God, and to seek his comfort for all who mourn. We particularly pray for God's restoring peace and loving presence with her children, the Princes William and Harry, and all her family.

In her life, Diana profoundly influenced this nation and the world. Although a princess, she was someone for whom, from afar, we dared to feel affection and by whom we were all intrigued. She kept company with kings and queens, with princes and presidents, but we especially remember her humane concerns and how she met individuals and made them feel significant. In her death she commands the sympathy of millions.

Whatever our beliefs and faith, let us with thanksgiving remember her life and enjoyment of it; let us rededicate to God the work of those many charities that she supported; let us commit ourselves anew to caring for others; and let us offer to him and for his service our own mortality and vulnerability.

All remain standing to sing

THE HYMN

I VOW to thee, my country, all earthly things above,
entire and whole and perfect, the service of my love
the love that asks no question, the love that stands the test,
that lays upon the altar the dearest and the best;
the love that never falters, the love that pays the price,
the love that makes undaunted the final sacrifice

And there's another country, I've heard of long ago
most dear to them that love her, most great to them that know;
we may not count her armies, we may not see her King;
her fortress is a faithful heart, her pride is suffering;
and soul by soul and silently her shining bounds increase
and her ways are ways of gentleness and all her paths are peace.

Thaxted   *Cecil Spring-Rice (1859-1918)*
Gustav Holst (1874-1934)

All sit, Lady Sarah McCorquodale reads:

IF I should die and leave you here awhile,
Be not like others, sore undone, who keep
Long vigils by the silent dust, and weep.
For my sake – turn again to life and smile,
Nerving thy heart and trembling hand to do
Something to comfort other hearts that thine,
Complete those dear unfinished tasks of mine
And I, perchance, may therein comfort you.

All remain seated. The BBC Singers, together with Lynne Dawson, Soprano, sing:

REQUIEM aeternam dona eis Domine, et lux perpetua luceat eis.
Libera me, Domine, de morte aeterna, in die illa tremenda quando

Outside Buckingham Palace.

The railings of Westminster Abbey almost disappearing behind thousands of tributes.

coeli movendi sunt, et terra: dum veneris judicare saeculum per ignem. Tremens factus sum ego et timeo, dum discussio venerit, atque ventura ira. Dies illa, dies irae, calamitatis et miseriae, dies magna et amara valde. Requiem aeternam dona eis Domine, et lux perpetua luceat eis.

R*EST eternal grant unto them, O Lord, and let perpetual light shine upon them. Deliver me, O Lord, from eternal death in that dread day when the heavens and the earth shall be shaken, and you will come to judge the world by fire.*
I tremble in awe of the judgement and the coming wrath.
Day of wrath, day of calamity and woe, great and exceeding bitter day.
Rest eternal grant unto them, O Lord, and let perpetual light shine upon them.

Guiseppe Verdi (1813-1901)
from The Requiem

All remain seated, Lady Jane Fellowes reads:

T IME is too slow for those who wait
too swift for those who fear
too long for those who grieve,
too short for those who rejoice,
but for those who love, time is eternity.

All stand to sing

THE HYMN

T HE King of love my Shepherd is,
whose goodness faileth never;
I nothing lack if I am his
and he is mine for ever.

Where streams of living water flow
my ransomed soul he leadeth,
and where the verdant pastures grow
with food celestial feedeth.

Perverse and foolish oft I strayed,
but yet in love he sought me,
and on his shoulder gently laid,
and home rejoicing brought me.

In death's dark vale I fear no ill
  with thee, dear Lord, beside me;
thy rod and staff my comfort still,
  thy cross before to guide me.

Thou spread'st a table in my sight;
  thy unction grace bestoweth:
and O what transport of delight
  from thy pure chalice floweth!

And so through all the length of days
  thy goodness faileth never
good Shepherd, may I sing thy praise
  within thy house for ever.

Dominus regit me   *H W Baker (1821-77)*
J B Dykes (1823-76)   *Psalm 23*

All sit. The Right Honourable Tony Blair, MP, Prime Minister, reads

1 CORINTHIANS 13

THOUGH I speak with the tongues of men and of angels, and have not love, I am become as sounding brass, or a tinkling cymbal. And though I have the gift of prophecy, and understand all mysteries, and all knowledge; and though I have all faith, so that I could remove mountains, and have not love, I am nothing. And though I bestow all my goods to feed the poor, and though I give my body to be burned, and have not love, it profiteth me nothing.

Love suffereth long, and is kind; love envieth not; love vaunteth not itself, is not puffed up, doth not behave itself unseemly, seeketh not her own, is not easily provoked, thinketh no evil; rejoiceth not in iniquity but rejoiceth in the truth; beareth all things, believeth all things, hopeth all things, endureth all things.

Love never faileth: but whether there be prophecies, they shall fail whether there be tongues, they shall cease; whether there be knowledge, it shall vanish away. For we know in part, and we prophesy in part. But when that which is perfect is come, then that which is in part shall be done away.

When I was a child, I spake as a child, I understood as a child, I thought as a child: but when I became a man, I put away childish things. For now we see through a glass, darkly; but then face to face: now I know

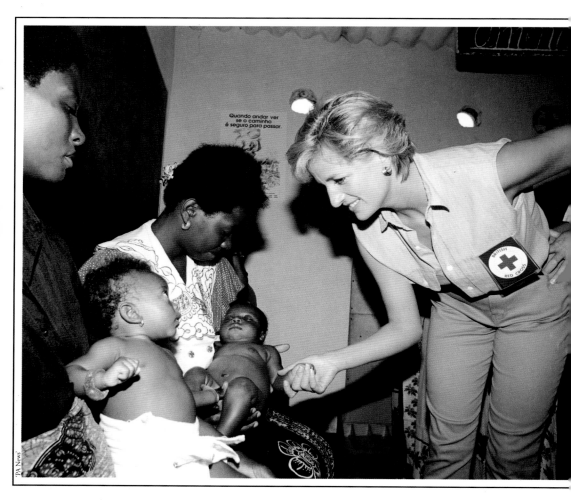

*In 1997, Diana, Princess of Wales visited Angola on behalf of the British
Red Cross in her campaign to abolish landmines. Her visit to the
victims drew world attention to the cause.*

'God made you special'.

The sea of floral tributes.

in part; but then shall I know even as also I am known. And now abideth faith, hope, love, these three; but the greatest of these is love.

All remain seated. Elton John sings

CANDLE IN THE WIND

GOODBYE England's rose;
    may you ever grow in our hearts.
You were the grace that placed itself
    where lives were torn apart.
You called out to our country,
    and you whispered to those in pain
Now you belong to heaven,
    and the stars spell out your name.

And it seems to me you lived your life
    like a candle in the wind:
never fading with the sunset
    when the rain set in.
And your footsteps will always fall here
    along England's greenest hills;
your candle's burned out long before
    your legend ever will.

Loveliness we've lost;
    these empty days without your smile.
This torch we'll always carry
    for our nation's golden child.
And even though we try,
    the truth brings us to tears;
all our words cannot express
    the joy you brought us through the years.

Goodbye England's Rose
    from a country lost without your soul,
who'll miss the wings of your compassion
    more than you'll ever know.

Bernie Taupin (b 1950)   *Elton John (b 1947)*

All remain seated for

188

THE TRIBUTE
by
The Earl Spencer

All stand to sing

THE HYMN

MAKE me a channel of your peace:
    Where there is hatred let me bring your love,
where there is injury, your pardon, Lord,
and where there's doubt, true faith in you:

> *O Master grant that I may never seek*
> *so much to be consoled as to console;*
> *to be understood as to understand,*
> *to be loved, as to love with all my soul!*

Make me a channel of your peace:
where there's despair in life let me bring hope,
where there is darkness, only light,
and where there's sadness, ever joy:

> *O Master grant that I may never seek*
> *so much to be consoled as to console;*
> *to be understood as to understand,*
> *to be loved, as to love with all my soul!*

Make me a channel of your peace:
it is in pardoning that we are pardoned,
in giving of ourselves that we receive,
and in dying that we're born to eternal life.

> *O Master grant that I may never seek*
> *so much to be consoled as to console;*
> *to be understood as to understand,*
> *to be loved, as to love with all my soul!*

Make me a channel of your peace:
where there is hatred let me bring your love,
where there is injury, your pardon, Lord,
and where there's doubt, true faith in you.

Sebastian Temple
arranged by Martin Neary (b 1940)

St. Francis of Assisi
translated by Sebastian Temple

189

'PA News'

As the Princess leaves Chicago's Cook County Hospital, in June 1996, sh
receives flowers and a hug from a young girl.

the end of her two-day visit to Bosnia to meet victims of landmines,
iana poses for a photographer with some French peace-keeping soldiers
Sarajevo Airport before her flight home to London in August 1997.

All sit. The Most Reverand and Right Honourable Dr. George Carey, Lord
Archbishop of Canterbury, Primate of all England and Metropolitan, leads

THE PRAYERS

For Diana, Princess of Wales

We give thanks to God for Diana, Princess of Wales; for her sense of joy
and for the way she gave so much to so many people.

LORD, we thank you for Diana whose life touched us all and for all
those memories of her that we treasure. We give thanks for those
qualities and strengths that endeared her to us; for her vulnerability; for
her radiant and vibrant personality; for her ability to communicate
warmth and compassion; for her ringing laugh; and above all for her
readiness to identify with those less fortunate in our nation and the world.

Lord of the loving; hear our prayer.

For her family

We pray for those most closely affected by her death: for Prince William
and Prince Harry who mourn the passing to their dearly loved mother;
for her family, especially for her mother, her brother and her sisters.

LORD, we thank you for the precious gift of family life, for all human
relationships and for the strength we draw from one another. Have
compassion on those for whom this parting brings particular pain and the
deepest sense of loss. Casting their cares on you, may they know the
gentleness of your presence and the consolation of your love.

Lord of the bereaved: hear our prayer

For the Royal Family

We pray for the Members of the Royal Family, for wisdom and
discernment as they discharge their responsibilities in the United
Kingdom, the Commonwealth and the world.

LORD, we commend to you Elizabeth our Queen, the Members of
the Royal Family and all who exercise power and authority in our

nation. Enrich them with your grace, that we may be governed with wisdom and godliness: so that in love for you and service to each other we may each bring our gifts to serve the common good.

Lord of the nations; hear our prayer.

For all who mourn

Diana was not alone in losing her young life tragically. We remember too her friend, Dodi Fayed and his family; Henri Paul, and all for whom today's service rekindles memories of grief untimely borne.

LORD, in certain hope of the resurrection to eternal life, we commend to you all who have lost loved ones in tragic circumstances. Give them comfort; renew their faith and strengthen them in the weeks and months ahead.

Lord of the broken-hearted: hear our prayer.

For the Princess' life and work

The Princess will be especially missed by the many charities with which she identified herself. We recall those precious images: the affectionate cuddle of children in hospital; that touch of the young man dying of AIDS; her compassion for those maimed through the evil of land mines – and many more.

LORD, we pray for all who are weak poor and powerless in this country and throughout the world; the sick, among them Trevor Rees-Jones; the maimed and all whose lives are damaged. We thank you for the way that Diana became a beacon of hope and a source of strength for so many. We commend to you all those charities that she supported. Strengthen the resolve of those who work for them to continue the good work begun with her.

Lord of the suffering: hear our prayer.

For ourselves

As we reflect on the Princess's compassion for others, we pray that we too may be inspired to serve as she served.

"To live in the hearts of those we leave behind is not to die."

Thomas Campbell 1777 – 184

The Prince of Wales and his sons Prince William (right) and Prince Harry, 'her beloved boys,' view the vast carpet of flowers and message of sympathy outside Kensington Palace, Princess Diana's London home

Outside Westminster Abbey.

LORD, we thank you for Diana's commitment to others. Give us the same compassion and commitment. Give us a steadfast heart, which no unworthy thought can drag down; an unconquered heart, which no tribulation can wear out; an upright heart, which no unworthy purpose can tempt aside. Grant us, O Lord, understanding to know you, diligence to seek you, wisdom to find you, and a faithfulness that may bring us to your eternal kingdom.

Lord of the compassionate: hear our prayer.

All remain seated. The Choristers sing:

> I WOULD be true, for there are those that trust me.
> I would be pure, for there are those that care.
> I would be strong, for there is much to suffer.
> I would be brave, for there is much to dare.
> I would be friend of all, the foe, the friendless.
> I would be giving, and forget the gift.
> I would be humble, for I know my weakness.
> I would look up, laugh, love and live.

Air from County Derry   *Howard Arnold Walter*
in G Petrie: The Ancient Music of Ireland (1853)

The Archbishop continues:

THEREFORE, confident in the love and mercy of God, holding a living faith in God's mighty resurrection power, we, the congregation here, those in the streets outside and the millions around the world, join one another and the hosts of heaven, as we say together, in whatever language we may choose, the prayer which Jesus taught us:

OUR Father, who art in heaven,
hallowed be thy Name.
Thy kingdom come,
thy will be done,
on earth as it is in heaven.
Give us this day our daily bread.
And forgive us our trespasses,
as we forgive those who trespass against us.
And lead us not into temptation, but deliver us from evil:
For thine is the kingdom, the power,
and the glory, for ever and ever. Amen.

The Archbishop says

THE BLESSING

THE God of peace who brought again from the dead our Lord Jesus, that great Shepherd of the sheep, make you perfect in every good work to do his will: and the blessing of God almighty, the Father, the Son, and the Holy Spirit, be with you and all whom you love, this day and for evermore. Amen.

All stand to sing

THE HYMN

GUIDE me, O thou great Redeemer,
pilgrim through this barren land;
I am weak, but thou art mighty;
hold me with thy powerful hand:
bread of heaven,
feed me now and evermore.

Open now the crystal fountain
whence the healing stream doth flow;
let the fiery cloudy pillar
lead me all my journey through:
strong deliverer,
be thou still my strength and shield.

When I tread the verge of Jordan
bid my anxious fears subside;
death of death, and hell's destruction,
land me safe on Canaan's side:
songs and praises
I will ever give to thee.

Cwm Rhondda   *W Williams (1717-91)*
John Hughes (1873-1932)   translated by P Williams (1727-96), and others

Standing before the Catafalque the Dean says

THE COMMENDATION

Let us commend our sister Diana to the mercy of God, our Maker and
Redeemer.

D IANA, our companion in faith and sister in Christ, we entrust you
    to God. Go forth from this world in the love of the Father, who
created you;
In the mercy of Jesus Christ, who died for you;
In the power of the Holy Spirit, who strengthens you.
At one with all the faithful, living and departed,
may you rest in peace and rise in glory,
where grief and misery are banished
and light and joy evermore abide. Amen.

All remain standing as the Cortège leaves the church, during which the choir sings:

A LLELUIA. May flights of angels sing thee to thy rest.
    Remember me O Lord, when you come into your kingdom.
    Give rest O Lord to your handmaid, who has fallen asleep.
    The choir of saints have found the well-spring of life, and door of
    paradise.
    Life: a shadow and a dream.
    Weeping at the grave creates the song:

Alleluia. Come, enjoy rewards and crowns I have prepared for you.

John Tavener (b 1944)   *extracts from William Shakespeare: Hamlet*
and the orthodox Funeral Service

At the west end of the church the cortège halts for the minute's silence observed by the Nation.

As a mark of respect to the Princess of Wales, the author would like to offer one of his favourite poems from the pen of Christina Rossetti.

REMEMBER

Remember me when I am gone away,
Gone far away into the silent land;
When you can no more hold me by the hand,
Nor I half turn to go yet turning stay.
Remember me when no more day by day
You tell me of our future that you planned:
Only remember me; you understand
It will be late to counsel then or pray.
Yet if you should forget me for a while
And afterwards remember, do not grieve:
For if the darkness and corruption leave
A vestige of the thoughts that I once had,
Better by far you should forget and smile
Than that you should remember and be sad.

Christina Rossetti 1830–94

It was a great honour for 'TFA' to be given ten places in Westminster Abbey for the service.

The Princess of Wales greeting Mother Teresa in New York.

"Sirena e vogël"
Tregim për Jonën e Vogël

Në qershor 1992 erdha në Shqipëri për herë të tretë dhe kësaj rradhe solla me vete një ekip mjekësh angleze.

Plani ynë ishte që të sillnim 20 fëmijë jetimë nga Jetimorja "Tefik Gyli" në spitalin e madh të Tiranës. Këta fëmijë vuanin nga sëmundje serioze të syve si glaukoma, katarakte, etj . . .

Pas dy ditësh tejet të vështira, të 20 fëmijët u operuan me sukses nga Dr. Nick Jaccobs nga Londra dhe nga Profesor Sulejman Zhungli nga Tirana.

Tre muaj më pas, kur u ktheva nëjetimoren "Tefik Gjyli", pashë se të gjithë fëmijët ishin në gjëndje shumë të mirë dhe e kishin marrë veten për mrekulli.

Pikërisht gjatë asaj vizite unë u njoha me Jehonën. ishte vetëm katër vjeçe dhe me flokët e saj kaçurrela të zeza ishte, për mendimin tim, vogëlushja më e bukur shqiptare që kisha parë. Fillova ta doja shumë, edhe ajo mua. Çdo herë që vija në Shqipëri për të sjellë ndihma humanitare, një nga gëzimet e vizitës sime ishte takimi me Jehonën.

Në fillim ajo mërzitej shumë kur ikja unë, por pak nga pak, pasi filloi ta kuptonte se unë do të vija përsëri, nisi të qetësohej.

Tani ajo është shtatë vjeçe dhe unë e kam takuar 19 herë. Ajo është larguar nga Jetimorja "Tefik Gjyli" dhe ka shkuar në një Jetimore për fëmijë me të rritur. Drejtori i kësaj jetimoreje është njeri i mrekullueshëm dhe e ka zgjedhur me shumë kujdes personelin e tij të shërbimit. Në udhëtimin tim të fundit, në qershor të këtij viti, ai më lejoi ta nxirrja Jehonën shëtitje.

Ishte një ditë e bukur vere dhe ne shkuam në liqenin e Shkodrës për të notuar. "Natyrisht që di not" më tha Jehona. Unë pata përshtypjen se ajo nuk dinte, dhe në fakt doli që kisha të drejtë. Ajo s'ishte futur ndonjë herë në ujë.

Ia kaluam për mrekulli. Më pas hëngrëm drekë në një anije që ishte restorant lundrues. Nuk mund ta merrni me mend shendin e saj kur po hanim drekë në anije!

Pasdite shkuam në kështjellën e Rozafës ku për dy tre orë eksploruam rrënojat e vjetra ilire dhe luajtëm një mori lojrash si "symbyllazi", etj.

Në orën 6.00 u kthyem në jetimore. Kishte qenë një ditë fantastike dhe ne i thamë njeritjetrit "lamtumirë" me dashuri. Kur pashë sytë e saj të mëdhenj, bojëkafe, të përlotur provova një ndjenjë dashurie shumë të madhe . . . për këtë vajzë shqiptare pa prindër. Ajo më buzëqeshi ëmbël e duke e ditur se unë do të kthehesha përsëri, dhe vërtet ashtu do të bëj.

Lidhjet e miqësisë midis mejepunonjës britanik i ndihmave dhe kësaj vajze nga jetime Shkodra u vendosën tri vjet më parë e tani janë forcuar më tepër se kurrë. Ndonëse asnjeri prej nesh nuk e flet gjuhën e tjetrit, të dy e dimë se çka në zemrën e secilit.

Përktheu: Marseda Shqarri.

20
THE LITTLE MERMAID

At the request of Shpresa Vreto, secretary of IBBY, The International Board on Books for Young People, I wrote the previous short story in simple words, which was translated into Albanian for inclusion in the children's magazine 'Sirena e Vogël', ('The Little Mermaid'). It tells of a rather special relationship, a different kind of love that reminded her nevertheless of Walt Disney's Ariel and Eric.

In June 1992 I returned to Albania for the third time and on this occasion took a team of English doctors with me.

The plan was to bring twenty orphan children from the Teufik G'yli orphanage in Shkodra to the No.1 hospital in Tirana. All the children had severe eye problems namely glaucoma, cataracts and squints.

After two very difficult days all twenty had been successfully operated on by Doctor Nick Jacobs from London and Professor Sulejman Zhugli from Tirana. On my return to Teufik G'yli three months later, I found all the children in good condition and fully recovered from their ordeal.

It was then I met Jehona for the second time. She was only four years old and with her dark curls was quite the most beautiful little Albanian girl I had seen. I became very fond of her and I think she of me, and each time afterwards when I subsequently visited Albania bringing humanitarian aid, one of the highlights of each visit would be my time spent with Jehona.

At first she was very upset when I left, but gradually when she realised I would come back, she came to accept the situation. Now she is seven years old and I have visited her nineteen times. She has left Teufik G'yli and gone to the orphanage for older children in Shkodra. The Director is a man of obvious integrity and chooses his staff carefully, and on our last trip in June 1995 allowed me to take Jehona out for the day.

It was a beautiful summer's day and together we went swimming in Lake Shkodra. "Of course I can swim," she gestured. I had a feeling she couldn't, and I was right – she had never been in water before.

We had a great time and this was followed by lunch on a floating restaurant. You can imagine her delight at eating on board a ship. In the afternoon we made our way to Rozafa Castle, where we spent several hours exploring the old Illyrian ruins and playing lots of fantastic games like hide and seek.

At 6.00 p.m. we made our way back to the orphanage.

It had been a wonderful day and we said our fond farewells.

Ariel

As I looked into her moist big brown eyes, I felt a tremendous feeling of love for this apparently unwanted child. She gave me a watery smile, but she knew I would be back.

Sirena e vogël – comment:

The bonds of friendship between the British aid worker and the orphan girl from Shkodra forged half her lifetime ago had become stronger than ever. Neither speaks the other's language, but both knew what was in the other's heart.

Jehona Metaliaj, destined to become the inspiration for the Albanian Charitable Foundation 'Child Smile', Buzeqeshja Feminore.

Jennie Linden

Jennie Linden, the British actress and film star provided the narration for 'TFA's recent video, in which Jehona's story was told for the first time.

Jennie is a very special lady.

*The smile that embodies all the hopes
and aspirations of Albania.*

21
JEHONA METALIAJ

With her mother dead, four year old Jehona together with her younger brother Lumi, were abandoned by their father in February 1992. He left them one bitterly cold morning tied to the gates of 'Teufik G'yli', Shkodra's only orphanage for young unwanted children.

His brief note, pinned to Jehona's torn, bloodstained jumper, said it all. "I don't want them – I'm going to Italy."

A week later I called at the orphanage for the first time, just prior to leaving Albania out of necessity. It was 'TFA's first mission and with the twenty juggernauts of aid safely delivered, the situation had become extremely volatile. Violence was erupting everywhere.

The eighty children at 'Teufik G'yli' had nothing – apart from a roof over their head. With little food, scant clothing and no beds, they slept, huddled together on the floor, comforted only by what little warmth they could generate from each other's bodies.

If ever there was a reason for us to return, then this was it.

As the children excitedly gathered round their unexpected guests, I was

The author's sons, Haydn (white cap) and Mansel (red T-shirt) befriending the orphaned children of Teufik G'yli in 1992. Five year old Jehona can be seen in the centre of the picture.

aware of a child hugging my left leg with all its might. I touched her hair with my left hand and as I did so, she turned and looked up at me. Our eyes met for the first time. Somehow, I knew this child was special – already, I could feel the tears welling up inside me and she was laughing and crying at the same time.

Our time at 'Teufik G'yli' was limited and our very presence had drawn a large crowd outside the gates – it was time to leave. I told Jehona I would be back, but she didn't understand.

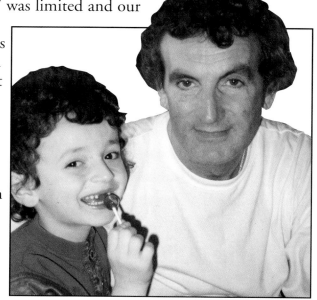

Over the next three years, I visited her nineteen times and our friendship steadily grew. She was moved to the orphanage for older children just prior to her eighth birthday and for a while things were fine. With the appointment of a new director, conditions deteriorated. Jehona was badly 'beaten up' by older boys on two separate

7th July 1994, Jehona enjoying her first birthday party at the age of seven.

occasions and with no anti-bacterial shampoo available, 'head lice' and 'nits' became a problem.

I had to do something to help her – but what?

Back in England, my own doctor was concerned for my well-being and sent me to see a psychotherapist. I was suffering from bouts of acute depression brought on by the Albanian situation.

There was so much to do out there, so many people who needed help. Watching people die, needlessly, especially premature new born babies through the lack of infant ventilators was heartbreaking. No matter where I went in Albania, 'everyone' – and I mean 'everyone,' wanted something. You couldn't blame them for asking – I was their only chance! It could be years before someone else came along.

It took eight weeks of treatment for me to fully realise that by focusing on the 'individual,' like Jehona, I could not help 'the majority.' Of course, being human I had feelings but I had to learn to protect myself by putting up mental barriers, thus remaining, to a degree, detached. It was a hard lesson to learn.

Often, life is about being in the right place at the right time and in September 1995, I was having coffee in the Tirana Hotel with the

Albanian authoress Shpresa Vreto. 'TFA' had just provided her with a four wheel drive Toyota to enable her organisation, 'Sirena e Vogël', ('The Little Mermaid') to distribute a children's magazine to rural and mountainous areas.

Somehow, Jehona's name came up in the conversation and I told her the child's story. For some reason, she was so enchanted with it, she asked if I could write it down and let her have a copy. Four weeks later, the article appeared on 'Sirena e Vogël's' front page and was read by thousands of children. One of the children who received the magazine passed it on to her mother. Fate had taken a hand, for this lady was the Vice Minister of Education. Some weeks later, an excited Shpresa telephoned me in England. "John, I know you are desperate to get Jehona out of that orphanage. Well, I think she is in luck."

March 1995, Jehona's last days at 'Teufik G'yli'.

The story unfolded.

Fifty years ago, an Austrian philanthropist by the name of Hermann Gmeiner, a medical student at the time, started an 'SOS village' in Vienna for orphaned and abandoned children. Today there are three hundred and sixty such villages worldwide and the latest has just been completed in Tirana.

Each village operates on the following four principles:

1)   Every child is given a mother – and she is theirs for life.
2) ....And a family of brothers and sisters...........................
3) ....And a home in a family house.....................................
4) ....In a village which is their bridge into the community at large.

The village also gives children the education and training they need to achieve independence.

It was the best news I had heard for ages!

The Vice Minister of Education a lifelong friend of Shpresa, was arranging to have Jehona and her brother transferred to the SOS village from Shkodra as soon as possible.

Jehona's story had touched her heart.

Finally, my long held dream for Jehona had come true. No more would she have to cry herself to sleep, in the pitch darkness, haunted by memories of being unwanted and unloved. Never again would she be shackled and tethered, inhumanely, like some animal.

At last she has a loving mother, six brothers and sisters and a village father who will always be there for her. The SOS concept, through world-wide sponsorship of its children, functions incredibly well. Being her sponsor, is a privilege I hold very dear.

It's a strange destiny that stalks Jehona Metaliaj. It's an even stranger fate that smiles on her, bestowing the rarest of Albanian gifts; one which has eluded her from birth – *a chance.*

June 1995 and Jehona enjoys her first 'day out' at Rozafa Castle.

"Love is an energy – if you give it, it will come back."

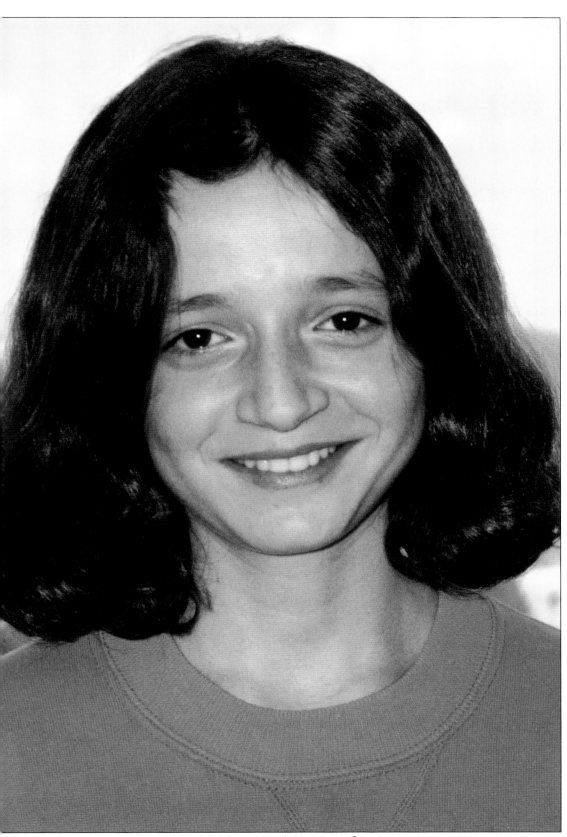

May 1998, growing up – fast.

211

22
THE 'GREMON' DISASTER

T he 'Gremon' sailed one morning in March 1997 from Durres. Its previous name was 'Anchorman' and both names had been registered with the Greek authorities in Athens, to where the ship was supposedly returning.

Once clear of port, *'the Captain, who was not a Captain,'* followed the coastline south for three miles, dropping anchor at a safe distance from the shore at Golem – he was expected.

Fifty refugees in search of a better life in Italy were to be taken on board and they would each pay one thousand dollars on arrival somewhere between Bari and Brindisi.

The beached 'Gremon'.

Scores of small boats left the beach in an attempt to reach the rusty freighter, their occupants clambering aboard as best they could with all their worldly possessions in tow.

Nine-hundred people made it onto the 'Gremon' and as the ship sank lower in the water, *'the Captain, who was not a Captain,'* pulled up the anchor. The weather had turned foul, a gale was blowing hard and within minutes, the 'Gremon' became stranded on a sand bar.

Realising the ship was listing badly and going nowhere, the refugees deserted, but not before stripping the freighter clean of everything portable.

The 'Captain' was never seen again – some say he went back to Athens. *Others say the Mafia insisted his nautical days were over.*

Whatever the truth, the 'Gremon' remains for all to see, like some beached whale, stranded helplessly. At night, under the full moon, its ghostly outline serves as a warning to all those contemplating departure.

A village elder pauses to say "thank you" for his 'box of clothing' before beginning the long walk home over the mountains.

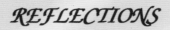

Carol Rowley amidst the poor but happy children of Qeshit, a remote village in eastern Albania.

A 'beggar baby' lies apparently abandoned on the Tirana pavement.

One of eight hundred thousand 'bunkers' built by Enver Hoxha to repel foreign invaders. This one guards the beach at Durres.

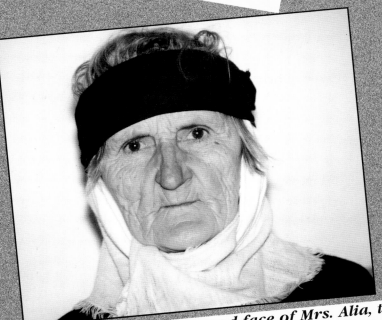

The proud face of Mrs. Alia, the mother of 'Jek Alia' the famous highlander from Malsia e Madhe.

June 1993, and ten year old Mansel van Weenen leaps from the aircraft steps, much to the annoyance of his elder brother Haydn, to become the first English boy to set foot on Albanian soil (well, concrete) for fifty years.

Whilst John was in West Bengal in February 1993 teaching the art of Karate-dō, he visited Mother Teresa in Calcutta. She was delighted to hear of his plans to hold a training seminar to which students from across the Indian sub-continent would be invited. As a mark of respect, the proceeds, in their entirety, would be donated to her Missionaries of Charity.

*'The smile that says it all.' Orphaned Anna,
thrilled with her new knitted hat.*

REFLECTIONS

A woman waits to have her baby in appalling surroundings at Koplik Hospital.

Sister Jose-Elaine (centre), pictured here with sisters from Tirana M.C. thanking 'TFA' for transporting a large consignment of aid from London.

Hey! forget about the eyes, what about the teeth?

Stephen Nash (right) at a dinner in January 1995, when he was the British chargé d'affaires to Albania. He left soon after but was welcomed back in June 1998 with much affection as H.M. Ambassador.

A reception room inside King Zog's Palace.

In June 1992, the author was joined by his wife Jane (right) seen here with Luiza and Thoma Dhamo.

'Far from the madding crowd.'
Back in England, John relaxes with his pride and joy – a 1959 Triumph T120 Bonneville.

24
MURDER ON THE MENU

Following on from the story of the 'Gremon,' only two hundred metres from where the big ship became stranded on a sand bar, stands the remains of the restaurant 'Anes Detit' (by the sea).

In May 1997, a most bizarre incident took place, which I shall recount exactly as it was told to me.

Three men had been drinking quite heavily since early morning in the restaurant of Tagir Okshtone, on the beach at Golem, just south of Durres. At 11.00 am they left by car for their homes in Kavaja.

The leader of the group, who was also the driver of the Mercedes they were travelling in, misjudged a bend in the road and the car hit a tree. The Mercedes was a write-off, although the three men were uninjured.

Returning to Golem alone, the leader, angry and drunk, confronted Tagir Okshtone.

In one hand he held a Kalashnikov, in the other a grenade. "Your 'Raki' was bad – it's given me a headache, and because of it my car is completely smashed. I want thirteen thousand dollars to pay for the car by tomorrow. If you have not got it then I shall kill you and destroy your restaurant."

The next day the three men returned to 'Anes Detit.' The leader, gun in hand, went into the restaurant, whilst his two confederates waited outside with a hand grenade.

'Anes Detit' being rebuilt after the grenade attack.

Tagir Okshtone said he had got the money and the gang leader was satisfied and signalled to his men outside. In reaching under the bar as if to get the cash, Tagir's hands locked onto his own Kalashnikov.

One shot rang out and the leader lay dead. His two friends made their escape but not before pulling the pin and throwing the grenade at the restaurant. 'Anes Detit' was badly damaged but fortunately, no one else was hurt.

In his anger at seeing his business destroyed, Tagir Okshtone unloaded his Kalashnikov into the head of the gang leader. There was nothing left to identify when the police arrived on the scene.

An official investigation revealed all three members of the gang were hardened criminals and although unnecessary force had been used on Tagir's part, massive provocation was evident and in the circumstances, no charges were brought against him.

I have included these two short stories as they both took place during the period of civil unrest in 1997.

Shpresa Vreto

Tatjana Zhugli

***Two special ladies who will be involved with the
National Children's Library project.***

25
THE GOOD SAMARITAN ENVER BRAHIMI 1963-1997

The Good Samaritan.

We had not witnessed, nor heard of a calamity for some time, but that was about to change. 'TFA's red Mazda van was following several trucks along the lonely mountain 'road' to Thethe. We had been advised the Mazda would cope admirably with the bad road, but after two hours driving, conditions became appalling.

No one saw the large jagged rock before we ran over it, but everyone heard it cut deeply through the engine sump like a knife through butter. A clean 'dipstick' was confirmed by a large puddle of oil in the gravel road.

It would be dark in an hour and with the safety of the aid in mind, we sent the trucks on to Thethe. Suddenly we were alone, with an engineless van and twilight approaching – our thoughts turned skyward.

'Let's go!'

We all three heard the sound of Enver Brahimi's truck at exactly the same time. With no thought for himself, The Good Samaritan, as he became known, towed us virtually all the way back using an old rusty chain that must have broken at least twenty times.

Finally, the chain was useless – it broke again for the last time. "You go first now," he said pointing into the black of night. "But how?" we enquired. "Gravity!" came the answer.

We were high up in the mountains with no engine, fading headlights and very little braking ability – we began to roll. Within minutes our speed was approaching 50 mph. With hindsight we couldn't have stopped if we had wanted to. At 60 mph, it became increasingly difficult to see in which direction the road had turned. The headlamp mainbeam was barely adequate and we were being bounced up and down like ping pong balls.

Enver Brahimi (centre front)
'A man for all seasons'.

Thirty minutes later, that seemed like an eternity, we 'arrived,' well – ground to a halt, one mile from the town of Koplik – miraculously intact. Fifteen minutes later, Enver caught us up.

As the moon rose behind us, we saw the outline of the mountain we had just 'driven' down. His strange Albanian sense of humour was lost on us when he muttered something about "Gravity being a very cheap fuel."

With a new chain, he proceeded to tow us all the way to Shkodra where Nail Gruda, a most ingenious mechanic, in a 'home made pit,' gas welded the entire sump to absolute perfection.

Enver Brahimi would not take one 'lek' from us for his trouble. The Enver Brahimis of this world are very special people.

That incident took place in November 1994 and since that time, we have come to know the Brahimi family well. After meeting Enver's mother and father, it was immediately obvious he had inherited their caring nature.

They were the most engaging couple and shared their house in Shkodra with Enver, his wife Mirjana and their two children. Ditmir was three years old, whilst his sister Brunilda was five. In the same house (and I'm not sure how) lived Enver's brother Shuajp, his wife Drita who speaks excellent English, and their daughters Besara and Fatjona.

Ingenuity beyond belief.

Shuajp was a policeman and occasionally when the Shkodra police were short of drivers, Enver would come to the rescue.

With the collapse of the Pyramid Saving Schemes in March 1997, conditions in Shkodra as elsewhere in the country became unstable. Violence erupted nationwide and armed gangs roamed the streets looting and killing indiscriminately.

The threat of civil war loomed but eventually, by May and June, had receded. The whole country awaited the General Election on 29th June 1997 when a predicted Socialist landslide was confirmed.

'Cold blooded murder of a Samaritan'

Less than four weeks later, on the evening of 25th July, Enver Brahimi had returned home from his police driving job, parked his vehicle outside his house, and walked the short distance to the 'Qemal Stafa' quarter.

He had arranged to meet a friend for coffee but as he waited for him, from out of the shadows came three masked men all wearing balaclavas.

They were unrecognisable.

Enver Brahimi had no chance. The gunmen, firing at random, hit Enver several times, one of the bullets lodged in his heart – he was dead before he hit the ground. In the space of a few seconds, it was all over. Three others were also injured before the gunmen disappeared into the alleyway from whence they came.

In October 1997 we visited the Brahimis. They were beside themselves with grief. Somehow, the house was different. Something vital was missing – we all knew what it was.

The Brahimi family in better times.
Left to right:
Enver, Mirjana, Mr. and Mrs. Brahimi, Drita and Shuajp.

'Thethe'

As Drita wrote in her letter to me in England "My heart is crying – Enver is no more".

His widow Mirjana is inconsolable. She feels her life is over too. For years to come she will wear black, use no make-up and probably never marry again, out of respect for her dead husband.

It is the Albanian way.

The passing of Enver has touched all of us in different ways but collectively, we feel remarkably privileged to have known him.

As I sat there enjoying the late autumn sun, writing these words in the comfort and safety of an English country garden, my thoughts were indeed far away.

Once again I heard the faint sound of Enver's truck breaking the silence of the mountain peaks.

I saw his broad smile and felt his warmth as his big hand clasped mine.

Two minutes earlier, I had prayed for help.

No words were spoken – it was not necessary.

I knew why he had come and he knew the part he must play in the scheme of things.

I thanked God for Enver Brahimi.

Postscript: April 1998

With spring only days away, I have spent many an hour during the long winter evenings here at 'The Priory,' reminiscing about the good times I had with Enver and his family.

How often, assuming you had been blessed with the gift of hindsight, would you have spent more time with someone, had you known their days were numbered?

What made you suddenly see them quite differently, so much nicer when they were no longer here? Why did it take their dying to bring into focus qualities you had previously been unaware of, or worse still – chosen to ignore.

Questions which I and many others often struggle to find an answer to.

Enver's work as a driver occasionally took him to the beautiful picturesque village of 'Thethe.' It lay hidden deep in a valley – a veritable 'Shangri-la,' high up in the remote Northern Albanian Alps.

It was here fate deemed our paths should cross and on meeting him, I sensed a certain contentment that came from within. On numerous occasions subsequently, he talked of his love for nature and the peace he had found. We shared the same interest in astronomy and his knowledge of the night sky was quite remarkable, equalled only by his insatiable appetite for poetry.

As a mark of respect to my dear friend, I have included an anonymous verse. The words could have been his and are appropriate in the extreme.

'*Do not Stand at my Grave and Weep*' was left in an envelope by Steven Cummings, a soldier killed on active service in Northern Ireland, to be opened in the event of his death. It was thought at first that the soldier himself had written it, but that was not the case.

Claims had been made it had come from nineteenth century magazines and had been a prayer of Navaho Indian Priests and this was possibly true. However, its origins remain a mystery.

DO NOT STAND AT MY GRAVE AND WEEP

—- o —-

Do not stand at my grave and weep;

I am not there. I do not sleep.

I am a thousand winds that blow.

I am the diamond glints on snow.

I am the sunlight on ripened grain.

I am the gentle autumn rain.

When you awaken in the morning's hush

I am the swift uplifting rush

Of quiet birds in circled flight.

I am the soft stars that shine at night.

Do not stand at my grave and cry;

I am not there. I did not die.

The well dressed people of 'Bushat' becoming extremely impatient for boxes of clothing, alas — for the worst possible reasons.

THE STRAW THAT BROKE THE CAMEL'S BACK

Wednesday 8th October 1997.

The thirtieth mission began in much the same way as most of those before it – with one exception. This time, the team were flying with Malev, the Hungarian airline, and were spending a day with John McGough in Budapest.

The 6.25 am flight out of Heathrow's Terminal Two must be the first of the day – I wonder if that's why it's the cheapest? The *last* time I had flown with Malev was in June 1992, my wife had joined me for her first trip – (and her last) to Albania.

I remember waiting by the baggage reclaim – a rusty trailer towed by an even more rusty

The inimitable John McGough.

tractor. As the cases came off, the pile got smaller. Somehow I just knew our baggage wasn't there! The Malev official had a very strange sense of humour. I thought he was joking at first – he wasn't.

"I've found your luggage sir – it's quite safe – problem is, it's in Bulgaria but don't you worry yourself, I'll get it here on the next plane." Today was Monday. "When is the next plane?" I enquired. "Friday said the official."

Existing on the contents of two cabin bags for four days was an experience.

At that time, it was impossible to get anything in Tirana as there were no shops. Friends gave up their half tube of toothpaste and lent us one worn down toothbrush. They also, ironically, lent us clothes that we had brought for them on the last mission.

However – I'm pleased to say, after five years, Malev had got their act together and after an 'enjoyable day' with John McGough in Budapest, we arrived in Albania on Thursday 9th October with luggage intact.

Bright and early the next morning, we met the thirty-eight tonne truck at Durres docks, completed customs formalities and headed north. Our destination was an impoverished area south of the city of Shkodra, in fact the zone of our old friend Pjeter Arbnori, the ex-'Speaker' of the Albanian Parliament.

It was composed of three villages with an estimated population of fifteen thousand people – Bushat, Barbullush and Ajmen.

Being our first trip since the ending of the conflict that had consumed that small beleaguered nation, a certain apprehension was evident and not without justification.

As our small convoy approached Bushat, with armed police officers fore and aft, the crowd gathered outside the compound gates were ecstatic. Once inside, the boxes of aid were distributed in an orderly way by village officials, who called for the 'head' of each household in turn.

A very happy Sister Maria-Garete at the M.C. Shkodra house receives two statues from London.

For two hours it all went well. Then it turned nasty. Not satisfied with one box, everyone wanted more. Fighting and arguing broke out and the police did nothing to stop it.

I moved our team back to a safe distance. A degree of order still prevailed but greed was on everyone's face. People didn't actually want the boxes for their contents, they just wanted them because *they were there*. By morning, an informed friend told us, "most of what you have brought will be on the black market."

Our 'TFA' group just sat back and watched the unfolding saga. We could not risk our lives and in the cold light of day, we were coming to terms with the reality of the situation.

No one spoke – there was no need, over six years of emergency aid had just come to an end.

It was time to move on.

In somewhat subdued mood we bade farewell to the empty truck, its driver and the token police escort as they made their way back to Durres.

The compound was deserted and apart from a few scattered empty cardboard boxes, nothing remained of the furore – it was as if it had never happened.

Our red Mazda van stood alone, loaded to the hilt with aid for Mother Teresa's Missionaries of Charity house nearby.

The sisters in London had asked us to deliver a consignment of aid to their counterparts in Shkodra. The people in the compound knew it was for 'the sisters,' yet made several attempts to steal it! *They had no shame.*

We drove out of the compound, turned right and headed north, on the short twenty kilometres journey to Shkodra.

The sisters were very pleased to see us and insisted on helping unload the thirty boxes of vital supplies, two statues and one very large crucifix. They were in buoyant mood despite the death of Mother Teresa on 5th September.

"She can help us much more now," said Sister Maria Garete, the head sister at the Shkodra house.

We marvelled at these women – utterly selfless, working tirelessly for the poor, each of whom own nothing more than two saris.

Sister Maria Garete was leaving for Tirana the following morning to meet Sister Nirmala, Mother Teresa's successor who had chosen Albania as the country for her first international visit.

It was indeed a real stroke of luck for us to have the opportunity to meet her and all the team found it a very humbling experience.

With thirty missions behind us involving the transportation of seven million pounds of aid, the time had come to change direction and move on to other things.

Sister Nirmala, who succeeded Mother Teresa as Superior General of the Missionaries of Charity.

In order to do this, 'TFA' had to apply to the Council and become an Albanian Non Governmental Organisation (NGO) and a Foundation within that country. Task Force Albania did not fare very well when translated into Albanian (in fact there are literally thousands of Task Forces all over the country) so it was decided after consultation with the lawyer to call the new Foundation 'Child Smile', Buzeqeshja Feminore.

Registration formalities were extensive, but finally on Tuesday 14th October 1997, a telephone call was received from our lawyers to say we had been successful.

There was much excitement as we met for dinner that evening, and it was fitting that our good friends Sulejman and Tatjana Zhugli and Socol and Lindita Agolli should join us. As I watched everyone eating, drinking and laughing, my thoughts drifted back to those dark days of 1991, when there were no restaurants, no shops, no cars and no hope.

In my mind's eye, I could see once again the orphanage in Shkodra and the seventy or so children dressed only in pants and vests, desperate for care and affection. Then there was Jehona, the beautiful, pathetic, five year old girl, with whom I formed an unbreakable liason and eventually with God's help was able to arrange for her and her natural brother to be brought to Tirana and installed in the beautiful Austrian SOS village and given their very own 'mother and father.'

In 1996, 'TFA' produced a video of its work for fundraising purposes. The film ended with a shot of a little girl with the most engaging smile imaginable. Virtually everyone who saw that video couldn't help remarking on that 'Child's Smile.'

It was only fitting that Jehona's smile should form part of our new charity logo, for in that smile was embodied all the hopes and aspirations of future generations.

Our biggest challenge was about to begin –
the building and creation of the **First National Children's Library of Albania.**

Registered in Albania as the N.G.O. and Foundation
'Buzeqeshja Feminore'

27
MICHAEL KENNEDY

O n 31st December 1997, New Year's Eve, Michael Kennedy was killed whilst skiing in Aspen, Colorado. The thirty-nine year old son of the late Senator Robert Kennedy, assassinated in 1968, was playing a game of 'catch' at the time, when he crashed into a tree. He died instantly of massive head and neck injuries.

Michael's death is the latest in a long line of tragedies for the Kennedy family. What has become known as the 'Curse of the Kennedys' had struck again. After the assassinations of John and Robert, Michael's own brother David, died of a drug overdose in Florida in 1984.

At the time of his death Michael was heading Citizens Energy Corp., a non profit organisation that supplied heating fuel to the poor. Indeed, a large part of his short life was given over to charity and good work of different kinds.

Michael Kennedy.

I remember well, meeting him for the first time. It was April 1993. I was escorting a consignment of medical aid into Tirana. After driving to the airport at Rinas in order to meet the Malev flight and collect the medicines, I parked the car and was about to enter the arrival lounge, when I heard a voice call "John." Looking round I was surprised to see the Minister of Health for Albania Dr. Tritan Shehu, who was gesturing for me to come over and join him.

He obviously knew why I was there, and taking my arm, we walked together through the VIP lounge and out on to the concrete runway. The Alitalia flight from Rome had also just landed and he was meeting someone important. A young man walked down the steps from the aircraft, who somehow looked vaguely familiar. Tritan shook hands with him and then turned to me, "Michael Kennedy, I'd like you to meet John van Weenen, a very good friend of mine."

As we walked back to the lounge for coffee, I admit to being a little shell shocked. Michael was very ordinary, down to earth and most interested in the work of 'TFA.'

That evening I was invited to an informal dinner at Enver Hoxha's villa in Tirana in honour of Michael and his first visit to Albania.

Stephen Nash, the British chargé d'affaires was present, as too was John McGough and Col. Cenan Cela. It was a most memorable evening and the only sad moment occurred when we raised our glasses to the memory of Michael's father.

The following day Michael joined us for dinner at the Dajti Hotel. We sat together and he asked me how I made a living when I wasn't bringing aid to Albania. When he discovered I had been a karate teacher for thirty years he was both surprised and excited. He had trained in Shotokan Karate himself in Boston and was the holder of a yellow belt.

He asked my grade, and when I said 6th Dan Black Belt, suddenly, I became his hero. It really was most embarrassing. Anyway, to cut a long story short, we got on 'like a house on fire,' and on parting, I gave him a signed copy of my latest karate book as he was so interested in the martial arts.

He was leaving Albania early the next morning but planned to return in the near future as he desperately wanted to help the country. We agreed to keep in touch by telephone, which we did and hoped to meet on his next visit to Albania.

That was the last I was to see of him, and as he left the hotel lobby, he turned and waved and I recognised that wonderful warmth of the Kennedy smile.

What a tragedy he was taken so young and we shall not see that smile again.

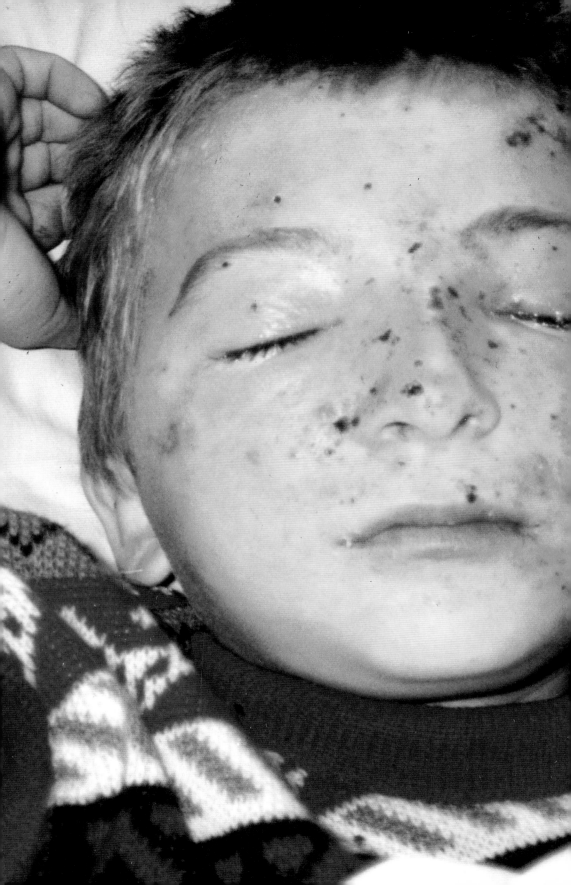

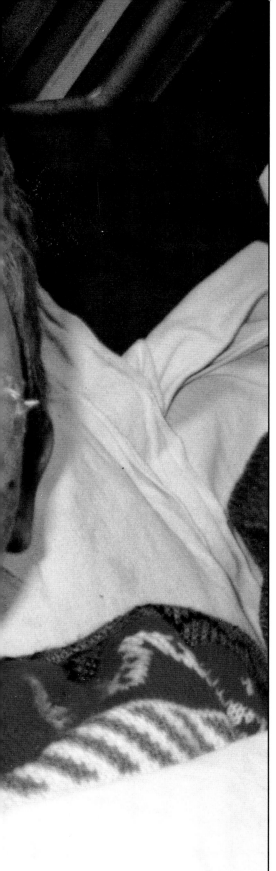

28

THE GAMES
CHILDREN
PLAY

Throughout the terrifying period of civil unrest between the months of February and July 1997, children of all ages could be seen on most city streets during daylight hours. In the south of the country especially, the Kalashnikov became a prized toy, but in most other areas, the children did what they do best – they played games.

As the rebellion came to a head, just prior to the General Election on 29th June, a new game emerged, that for many, proved to be a fatal attraction. In an odd way, they were 'muscling in' on the adults' action. Not content with 'tag' or 'hide and seek', they devised a new method of entertaining themselves that consisted of, initially, collecting as many rounds of live ammunition as possible. The next stage of the game required the participants to each take a live shell and ram it, point first, into the soft earth until only the base of the bullet was visible and more pertinently, the small circle in the centre, normally reserved for the firing pin.

Finally would come the 'pièce de résistance.' The children would take it in turns to throw sharp stones at their bullet. Whichever exploded first was the winner – or sadly, the loser.

On January 11th 1998, in the town of Berat, thirteen year old Jonin Bega had carefully pushed 'his' live Kalashnikov shell into the ground. It had been raining that morning so only slight pressure was needed to make a suitable hole. He waited patiently for his turn to come and watched intently as his two friends both failed to ignite their shells.

Now it was his turn.

With almost uncanny precision, Jonin's aim was 'perfect.' The shell exploded but instead of forcing the projectile downwards as he had assumed would happen, the exposed end, with nothing to prevent it from doing otherwise, flew up and smashed into his face!

In an instant, Jonin Bega was blinded, and will be so *for the rest of his life.*

On hearing of their son's accident, the family immediately drove him the one hundred kilometres to Tirana and carried him still bleeding profusely into the ophthalmological ward of the University Hospital. Dr. Lindita Agolli, one of Albania's top anaesthetists and a long time friend of 'TFA' was on duty and within minutes she summoned her fellow doctors.

Sadly, there was very little anyone could do.

Jonin's eyes had been destroyed.

They could only bathe him, relieve the pain, and pray.

Jonin had become Albania's latest statistic.

We all hoped he would be the last, but in our hearts – we knew he wouldn't be.

29
TASK FORCE ALBANIA CHILD SMILE (BUZEQESHJA FEMINORE) SYNOPSIS

October 1991 – 1st Mission:
Initial visit by the author at the invitation of Dr. Sali Berisha to assess the situation.

January 1992 – 2nd Mission:
Twenty juggernauts leave Britain loaded with food and clothing.
The largest aid convoy to leave Britain since World War Two.

April 1992 – 3rd Mission:
Visit to make all arrangements for the arrival of British doctors in Albania.

May 1992 – 4th Mission:
Team of doctors fly to Albania to perform complicated eye surgery on twenty orphaned children.

May 1992 – 5th Mission:
Clothing and children's medicines to orphanages in Shkodra.

June 1992 – 6th Mission:
Jet ventilator to Intensive Care Unit at Tirana Hospital. Request of Minister of Health

September 1992 – 7th Mission:
Aid to Tirana and escorting of three leading Albanian doctors to London.

October 1992 – 8th Mission:
Survey of all hospitals in the Great Highlands of Albania.

November 1992 – 9th Mission:
Aid to the commune of Bajze.

January 1993 – 10th Mission:
Warm clothing and bedding to Tirana, Koplik and Bajze.

Derek Barnett in October 1992 bringing food and clothing to the starving people of northern Albania

April 1993 – 11th Mission:
Snow melts. Aid to the far north of Albania to the villages of Tomara and Vermosh.

July 1993 – 12th Mission:
Discussions and meetings in Tirana. Visit to Vlora.

September 1993 – 13th Mission:
Five hundred Rotary boxes to Bajze. Dentistry equipment to Koplik.

October 1993 – 14th Mission:
Aid to Berat, Vlora, Shkodra and villages in Kruma district.

November 1993 – 15th Mission:
Three trucks including five hundred Rotary boxes to warehouse in Durres. Aid from Mother Teresa's home in London to Shkodra.

February 1994 – 16th Mission:
Empty warehouse in Durres. Twelve military trucks to Shkodra with fifty per cent to northern villages.

May 1994 – 17th Mission:
Visit Vermosh and ten villages of the Kelmendi region with one thousand Rotary boxes. Aid to Bajze school and medical centre.

September 1994 – 18th Mission:

Two hundred thousand pounds worth of medical equipment to Tirana hospital.
Forty thousand pounds worth of educational aid to Koplik. Delivery of Mazda van.

November 1994 – 19th Mission:

One thousand Rotary boxes to Thethe and other villages.
Three hundred and fifty thousand pounds worth of antibiotics to the Ministry of Health in Tirana.

January 1995 – 20th Mission:

Visit with Norman Wisdom.
Exploratory talks with regard to

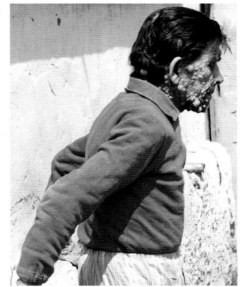

No cure in sight – no place to hide.

building a medical clinic in Tirana in conjunction with four other British charities – Feed the Children; ADRA; Child Hope and Jersey Aid.

March 1995 – 21st Mission:

One thousand boxes of clothing to Librazsd in central eastern Albania.
Feasibility study undertaken to give assistance to one hundred and thirty-eight thousand destitute people in sixty mountain villages.

'Knights of Old' trucks arriving by ferry at Durres laden with humanitarian aid.

June 1995 – 22nd Mission:

Delivery and installation of two paediatric ventilators to Tirana's maternity hospital. Total value of forty thousand dollars.
Search for missing pilots killed in 1944.
Meetings in Tirana with Government officials to make arrangements for September convoy.

September 1995 – 23rd Mission:

Transportation and safe delivery of ten thousand family boxes to the city of Librazsd in central eastern Albania.
Delivery of a four-wheel drive Toyota car to the Albanian Children's Association 'The Little Mermaid,' for transporting educational material to remote mountain areas.

October 1995 – 24th Mission:

Clothing and medical aid delivered with the help of the Albanian military (twenty truck convoy) to the remote villages in eastern Albania close to the border with Macedonia.

December 1995 – 25th Mission

Three thousand children's Christmas boxes safely distributed in the region of Librazsd.

May 1996 – 26th Mission:

Two juggernauts containing medical aid to Peshkopia Hospital and Dibra.

May 1996 – 27th Mission:

Preparations for 28th Mission
Invitation to John van Weenen for General Election.

November 1996 – 28th Mission:

Major consignment of aid to Peshkopia region.

August 1997 – 29th Mission:

Visit by John van Weenen to assess the new situation in Albania after the rebellion and change of government.

October 1997 – 30th Mission:

Winter clothing to Bushat, Barbullush and Ajmen.
Transfer of aid from London to Shkodra for Missionaries of Charity.
Registration and legal formalities of new Albanian Foundation 'Child Smile.'
Talks and feasibility study regarding the First National Children's Library of Albania.

January 1998 – 31st Mission:

Transportation and delivery of the remaining aid from our Bedford warehouse to the north eastern city of Peshkopia.

High level meetings over a period of four days with the Ministry of Education, the Ministry of Culture and the Mayor of Tirana to discuss the creation of Albania's First National Children's Library.

Site meetings scheduled with all interested parties.

Transfer of aid from Mother Teresa's home in London to Tirana.

Postscript
The following extract was written at the end of 1994.

Task Force Albania has also sent considerable consignments of aid to the following cities, towns and villages:

Tirana, Shkodra, Kavaja, Bajze, Koplik, Kruma, Thethe, Tomara, Vermosh, Hani Hoti, Lepusha, Selca, Broja, Kozhnje, Vulke, Nikci, Bratoshe, Kastrat, Breglumi, Lotaj, Shoshi, Pulti, Sukaj, Boga, Dedaj and Vuksanaj.

In addition to this, a pilot scheme to supply Albania's top surgeons with reliable four wheel drive vehicles got underway. The first vehicle arrived in October and Professor Sulejman Zhugli, head of Albania's Ophthalmological Society, took possession. It will enable him to visit outlying villages and hospitals to perform eye surgery whilst, at the same time, giving seminars and advice to junior doctors.

Thanks to Mr. Hekuran Skuqi, the Director of State Reserves, a government warehouse was placed at our disposal in the port of Durres. With a firm base to work from Task Force Albania has now begun to stockpile essential items, ready for delivery by the military to selected towns and villages where there is the greatest need.

And so it goes on. Perhaps 1995 will be the year when the Bosnian conflict will be resolved and the axe hanging over Albania's head will be lifted. In the meantime, its fragile economy struggles for survival. The investors have come and gone, and sadly – few have returned.

This tiny Balkan nation desperately needs a lucky break, for it had the courage to shake off the bonds of communism that had imprisoned it for almost fifty years. After all that, how ironic its own destiny should lie 'just out of reach,' and in the hands of others.

30
FUNDRAISING – THE NGOs' NIGHTMARE

S ooner rather than later, Non Governmental Organizations (NGOs) are forced to address the unavoidable fact, that in order to survive, they need 'money' — and in considerable amounts at that.

Many groups begin life for the best reasons, often motivated by nothing more than a desire to help. Sustaining that effort beyond the short term, calls for financial stability. Funding is usually the biggest problem facing voluntary organisations. With so many good causes, all equally deserving in their own way, there is unfortunately, only 'so much money' to go around.

Donors have the difficult job of deciding whom to give it to, for what, and how much.

The majority of funding comes from one of the following areas: trusts, companies, associations, business, governmental departments,

'Maria' director of the orphanage 'Teufik G'yli' surrounded by her 'family' all wearing their new knitted hats courtesy of the Ladies of the Inner Wheel clubs of Great Britain and Ireland.

foundations and individuals. For organisations with similar aims to 'TFA,' approaches may be made to: The European Union, The Phare Programme, The Know How Fund, The Department for International Development (DFID), The National Lottery, and the East European Partnership, to name just a few.

Throughout my years involved in the charity world, I have to confess to finding some groups 'less than forthcoming' with information relating to fundraising. Charities are not always 'that charitable,' when it comes to divulging the source of their income. No doubt it is naive of me to imagine they would act otherwise.

That aside, hopefully 'TFA' has always endeavoured to offer help and assistance to any individual or charitable group who has made an approach. With that sentiment in mind, knowing how difficult it is for any new group to flourish, I offer, if it is not too presumptuous, a brief resumé of 'TFA's most recent appeal.

Once having decided on the right project (The National Children's Library of Albania - October 1997), I returned to England, convened a meeting and discussed my ideas with 'TFA's small group of volunteers. I hoped it would receive unanimous approval, which it did, for the change from humanitarian aid to development was a natural progression.

Only six people sat around the table and the absence of any others highlighted 'TFA's main problem. Without an army of volunteers, little could be done, we needed to involve large groups of people in order to raise the three hundred and eight thousand pounds necessary to build the library.

A plan of action was formulated.

With money and books being the essential items, a simple scheme was devised to 'kill two birds with one stone,' it became known as 'A Book and a Pound' and the following groups were written to.

1) Two hundred education authorities in Great Britain and the twenty five thousand head teachers in their employ.

2) The sixteen hundred clubs of Rotary International in Great Britain and Ireland.

3) Eleven thousand secretaries of the Association of Inner Wheel Clubs of Great Britain.

4) The five thousand wealthiest people in the country.

5) Three thousand grant making trusts who consider making donations to educational and overseas projects.

Additional applications were also made for funding to The National Lottery, The Fire Service, The Princess of Wales Trust and The Know How Fund. Disappointing replies were received from The Fire Service, Lions Clubs International, The Police Force, The Association of Round Table Clubs, Women's Institutes (W.I.) and The Scout Association, all of whom could not, due to their structure, support us at national level. Most suggested contacting their local clubs and branches direct, which for 'TFA,' would have been a statistical impossibility.

The media were contacted and Press releases issued to all national newspapers and television companies. Individual approaches were made to prominent radio programme presenters, BBC's Blue Peter and DFID (formally ODA).

Five months into the scheme, seventy five thousand books have been delivered to 'TFA's R.A.F. Cardington warehouse and funds are accumulating steadily.

Lessons learnt.

The 'book and a pound' scheme was an excellent idea. However, most people in their generosity chose to give more than one book, in fact several, but – minus the additional pounds!

Transportation costs to Albania rocketed.

We 'very kindly' suggested to participating schools, that should they find themselves 'strapped for cash,' it would be quite in order to deduct the postage costs of sending the books to the warehouse from the sum of the pounds collected. The obvious psychology was to encourage them to 'take part.' With hindsight that was a mistake!

Conclusions.

In a crisis, people will always want to help and ordinary individuals will follow their conscience and take matters into their own hands.

When Albania opened its doors after forty seven years' of communism and the first horrifying pictures were shown on British television, countless Britons downed tools, hired Ford Transit vans, filled black bin liners with warm winter clothing, loaded them and headed for Dover.

Many didn't make it. The road to Albania was littered with broken down vehicles and drivers in possession of invalid documents. Some reached the German border, but fewer still made it to Czechoslovakia, Hungary and Yugoslavia. The war in Serbia had claimed many a casualty, not least of all our intrepid 'transit van driver' metaphorically speaking, who was included in that number. Only a handful reached their destination relatively unscathed and 'TFA' with twenty juggernauts was very, very lucky to do so. Without some divine help, we could never have done it.

I suppose in doing something perfectly, one learns very little, but doing it badly can be a great learning experience. If nothing else, I learnt on that trip the importance of planning, logistics and funding, and without the latter, the former remains a paper exercise.

Neglect fundraising at your peril!

The crowd in Skanderbeg Square await the result of the General Election on May 26th 1996.

31
THE POLITICAL QUAGMIRE

The 'Hoxha Experiment'

At first closely allied with Yugoslavia, Albania backed the Soviet dictator Stalin in his 1948 dispute with the Yugoslav ruler Tito and developed close links with the USSR in 1949-55, entering the trade organisation Comecon in 1949. Hoxha imposed a Stalinist system with rural collectivisation, industrial nationalisation, central planning, and one-party control. Mosques and churches were closed in an effort to create the 'first atheist state.' Hoxha remained a committed Stalinist and broke off diplomatic relations with China in 1978. The 'Hoxha Experiment' left Albania with the lowest income per head of population in Europe. After Hoxha's death in 1985, there was a widening of external economic contacts and the number of countries with which Albania had formal diplomatic relations increased from seventy-four in 1978 to one hundred and eleven in 1988.

Open Dissent

Opposition to the regime began to mount during 1990. In early July unprecedented anti-government

Violence E.

Riot police are called out during a protest against the Pyramid Savings Schemes in Skanderbeg Square, Tirana on 18th January 1997.

Protest in Tirana on 26th January 1997.

with the collapse of the

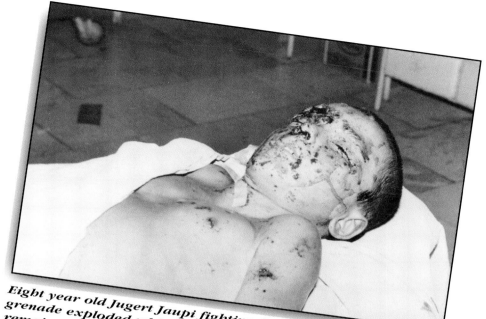

Eight year old Jugert Jaupi fighting for life after a hand grenade exploded while the family were sifting through the remains of their house on 3rd June 1997.

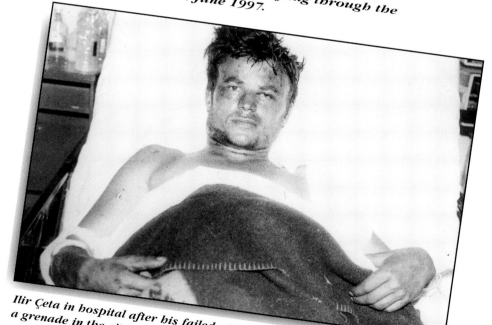

Ilir Çeta in hospital after his failed attempt to kill President Berisha with a grenade in the city of Durres on 4th June 1997.

ramid Savings Schemes'

street demonstrations erupted in Tirana. Faced with a government crackdown, five thousand demonstrators sought refuge in foreign embassies and were later allowed to leave the country. Later the same month diplomatic relations with the USSR were restored and embassies re-established.

Reminiscent of a film set from 'Quatermass' or 'Terminator,' this state owned copper producing factory closed in 1997. It stands derelict by the roadside in the town of Laç; a sinister reminder of Albania's communist past.
Even today, the stench of sulphuric acid fills the air and leakage into the streams and rivers has become a major health hazard to humans and animals alike.

End of One-Party System

In December 1990, amid continuing protests in Tirana and economic collapse, the communist party leadership announced that the existence of opposition parties had finally been authorised and the ban on religion lifted. An opposition party was immediately formed by the Tirana intelligentsia: the Democratic Party (DP), led by Sali Berisha. Elections (secret ballot) to the People's Assembly due to be held in February 1991 were postponed to give the new party some time to organise, and in return the opposition agreed to a temporary wage freeze and ban on strikes.

May 26th 1996. President Sali Berisha wins his second General Election for the Democratic Party.

Civil Unrest

A huge bronze statue of Hoxha in Tirana was toppled by demonstrators in February 1991, and there were riots in several other towns. President Alia replaced the unpopular premier Adil Carcani with Fatos Nano, a reform economist. Alia also declared the imposition of presidential rule and tanks were moved into the streets of Tirana. Fears of a right-wing coup prompted a flight of thousands of Albanians to Greece, Yugoslavia and Italy. 'Non-political' refugees were sent back to Albania.

First Multi-party Elections

Diplomatic relations with the USA and the UK, suspended since 1946, were restored in March and May 1991 respectively. In Albania's first free multi-party elections, held March - April 1991, the ruling Party of Labour of Albania (PLA) captured one hundred and sixty-nine of the two hundred and fifty seats in the new People's Assembly. It secured sufficient seats for the necessary two thirds majority to make constitutional changes.

PLA came predominantly from rural areas. In the major towns the DP, which captured seventy-five seats, polled strongly, convincingly defeating President Alia in the first round in the Tirana constituency. The frustration of the opposition's supporters was vented in anti-communist rioting in Shkodra on 6th April 1991, with four persons being shot dead by the police, including the local DP leader. The report of a commission subsequently blamed the security forces for these deaths and the Sigurimi (secret police) were replaced in May 1991 by a new National Security Council.

Protest in Tirana on January 26th against 'Sudja,' the 'Gypsy Queen,' whose Pyramid Savings Scheme collapsed with debts of forty million dollars.

Economic Problems

An interim constitution was adopted in April 1991, with the country renamed the Republic of Albania and the PLA's leading role being abandoned. The new People's Assembly elected Ramiz Alia as both the new Executive President of the republic, (replacing the Presidium), and Commander-in-Chief of the armed forces. In May 1991 Fatos Nano was re-appointed Prime Minister, but resigned in June. The economy deteriorated rapidly: agricultural, industrial products, and exports were declining and unemployment stood at almost forty per cent. Nano was replaced by Ylli Bufi, the former food minister, heading a new, interim 'Government of National Stability' with members from the opposition parties, including Gramoz Pashko (DP leader) as Deputy Premier. In June 1991 the PLA renamed itself the Socialist Party of Albania (PSS), with Fatos Nano elected as its chair. In July 1991 a Land Privatisation Bill was passed to restore land to peasants dispossessed under communist rule. From late summer 1992 Albania began to receive emergency aid from the European Community (now the European Union). Between September and December 1991 there were recurrent anti-communist demonstrations, bread riots, and protest strikes prompted by deteriorating living conditions and continued attempts by Albanians to leave the country.

First Non-communist Leaders

The DP withdrew from the coalition government claiming that it was being manipulated by former communists, and on December 6th 1991 Prime Minister Bufi resigned. On December 18th 1991 President Alia appointed Vilson Ahmeti, a former nutrition minister, as Albania's first non-communist Premier.

In January 1992 twenty former Albanian communist officials were arrested on corruption charges. The DP won sixty-two per cent of the national vote in March 1992 elections against twenty-five per cent for the PSS. The newly formed parliament elected Sali Berisha, founder and leader of the DP, as the country's President and granted him increased executive powers. Alexander Meksi succeeded Ahmeti as Prime Minister. In 1992 a ban was imposed on all 'facist, anti-national, chauvinistic, racist, totalitarian, communist, Marxist-Leninist, Stalinist or Enverist (following Enver Hoxha)' political organisations and in September former President Ramiz Alia was charged with abuse and misuse of power and misuse of state funds. In January 1993 Nexhmije Hoxha, the widow of Enver Hoxha was sentenced to nine years imprisonment for misuse of government funds between 1985-90.

Chaos

The economic situation continued to decline, with half the workforce unemployed, inflation out of control and agriculture in a state of paralysis with disagreements over land ownership. In the face of increasing lawlessness, the United Nations intervened to help reorganise the police force and curb drug trafficking.

From 1993-1996 economics and living standards improved and Albania became a member of the Council of Europe. Berisha's political opponents in the meantime accused him of being autocratic. Nevertheless, he failed to control the 'Pyramid Savings Schemes' which collapsed in January 1997 and resulted in the country being thrown into widespread chaos and anarchy.

The DP conceded defeat to the Socialist Party (SP) on 29th June 1997 winning only twenty-four of the one hundred and fifty-five seats contested. The SP won one hundred. Dr. Rexhep Mejdani was elected President and Fatos Nano became Prime Minister.

President Rexhep Mejdani with the author in May 1998.

The Albanian Ambassador to Great Britian, His Excellency Agim Fagu.

32
MARY EDITH DURHAM

Throughout my travels in Malsia e Madhe (The Great Highlands of northern Albania) when it became known I was English, the name of Edith Durham would crop up time and time again. Her name was always spoken with great admiration and respect.

She spent many years in the early part of the twentieth century roaming and exploring the Balkans. As an authoress she was prolific and her knowledge and understanding, especially of the tribal people of northern Albania has never been equalled by anyone.

Her documentation of the 'Canoni' or Tribal Law is historic and her research and translation into the canon of Lek Dukagin remains invaluable.

A fellow of the Royal Anthropological Institute in London, the works of Edith Durham include: High Albania, Twenty Years of Balkan Tangle, The Sarajevo Crime and Some Tribal Origins, Laws and Customs of the Balkans.

In 1912 along with Col. Aubrey Herbert she formed the Anglo Albanian Association which still meets today in London. In 1993, I was asked to become its vice-president and accepted most gladly. On November 28th every year it hosts an Albanian Independence Day celebration party in central London which is always very well attended.

Mary Edith Durham was a great Englishwoman, anthropologist, authoress and traveller, a lady held in the highest regard by Albania and its people.

Testimony to that was highlighted when towards the end of her life King Zog awarded her 'The Order of Skenderbeg.' She died in London in 1944 and three years earlier gave a special afternoon lecture on Tuesday 4th February 1941 to the Royal Institution of Great Britain.

That lecture was entitled simply 'Albania' and I am most grateful to Mr. Dervish Duma of the Anglo-Albanian Association in London for supplying me with a draft copy which now follows:

I would plead for justice for one of the oldest and now one of the most unfortunate peoples of Europe. Sympathy is warm for the Poles but the Albanians, who have suffered yet more brutal dismemberment at the hands of their more powerful neighbours, are now the battlefield of two rival Powers and threatened with annihilation in a quarrel which is not their own.

The Albanians are descended from the tribes who dwelt in prehistoric times along the western side of the Balkan peninsula – the Illyrians and the Epirots – before the arrival of either the Romans or Slavs. They were not and are not Greeks.

Strabo, writing about the beginning of the Christian era, gives details which show that their tribal system resembled that which has existed until recent times. He states that the frontier of the Greeks was south of the Ambracian Gulf, now the Gulf of Arta. That is further south than today. Albanian territory was taken by the Greeks in 1913. The Illyrians and the Epirots are now known as the Ghegs and Tosks. They speak the same language, have the same customs and form a united nation.

When Rome conquered the Balkan peninsula, Christianity reached the Adriatic coast and Illyria formed part of the Patriarchate of Rome. When the decline and fall of the Roman Empire began Roman rule was replaced by Slav rule, the peninsula was invaded by the ancestors of the modern Serbs and for a short time in the Middle Ages they ruled a large part of it.

A contemporary account by the Dominican, Father Brocardus, 1331, shows the Abbanois, as he calls them, speaking their own language clinging to their Church and 'very harshly oppressed' by their conquerors. The laws enacted by the Serb Tsar Stefan Dushan in 1349 show that they were classed as herdsmen serfs. The Serb Empire was short-lived. At its greatest it lasted but twenty-five years – the reign of Stefan Dushan. On his death the conquered peoples and rival chieftains speedily broke it up and the inrush of the Turks destroyed it completely. Meanwhile the Venetians had crept down the coast. Albanian chieftains rose to power in the mountains; together with the Venetians they long defended Scutari which finally fell in 1478. But the Albanians were the last of the Balkan peoples to be subdued. Led by their great hero Skenderbeg, famed as the champion of Christendom, they offered a magnificent resistance from his stronghold at Kruja. On his death of the fever in 1467 they were leaderless and forced to accept Turkish suzerainty. Their position differed from that of the other conquered peoples as they retained a semi-independence under their own chiefs. Race instinct, that blind unreasoning instinct of self-preservation, drew them against their old oppressor and they sided with the Turks in an endeavour to expel the Serbs. The position of the Serbs in the Kosovo district was made untenable. Led by the Bishop of Ipek they migrated en masse into lands in Hungary allotted them by the Emperor. The Albanians re-occupied the lands from which their ancestors had been evicted and retained them till 1913.

Turning Moslem in considerable numbers the courage and intelligence of the Albanians enabled them to rise high in the Turkish army and

Government. As did the Roman and the Serbian Empires, so did the Turkish Empire reach its zenith and wane. Towards the beginning of the nineteenth century the subject peoples began to think of independence. Ali Pasha, a mighty chief in South Albania, born at Tepeleni in 1744, revolted, defied the Turks and for some fifty years ruled all South Albania from his capital at Janina; entered into diplomatic relations with Great Britain and France and received many distinguished visitors, notably Lord Byron and Sir Henry Holland. In his old age he was overpowered by large Turkish forces and his head was carried to Constantinople as a trophy in 1822. I found his name still honoured when I was at Tepeleni in 1904.

Meanwhile Russia fixed greedy eyes on Constantinople and incited and aided Greeks, Serbs and Bulgars to revolt. The Greeks, aided also by Great Britain, were the first to recover independence and be given a foreign king. In 1876-77 came the Russo-Turkish war to liberate the Slavs. Again the Albanians sided with the Turks and put up a very strong resistance to Serb invasion, defending their towns of Djakova, Prizren and Prishtina successfully. Turkish resistance broke at Plevna. There followed the Treaty of Berlin and the Eastern Roumelian Commission. Much wholly Albanian land was allotted to the Serbs, Montenegrins and Greeks. The Albanians formed the League of Prizren, summoned their forces and saved much of it. The northern tribesmen kept the Montenegrins out of Gusinje. I knew fine old Marash Hutzi of Hoti who organized the defence. Dulcigno, a purely Albanian town and Antivari, inhabited solely by Moslem and Catholic Albanians, were handed over to Montenegro. The Janina district, however, was saved from the Greeks and Kosovo from the Serbs.

At this time Lord Goschen and Lord Fitzmaurice on the Eastern Roumelian Commission, strongly favoured forming a large and independent Albania to include all Janina vilayet, all Kosovo vilayet and a considerable part of Macedonia. Lord Fitzmaurice took very great interest in Albania and corresponded with me about it for some fifteen years. He maintained that had an Albanian state been then formed both the Balkans and Europe would have been spared much bloodshed; each of the respective peoples would have had a fair share and balanced each other. But the prejudice against Moslems was then too strong.

I became interested in the Albanian question in 1903. A revolt of the Bulgars of Macedonia who wished to join free Bulgaria was sharply suppressed by the Turks, leaving a mass of burnt villages and starving people. As I had done much Balkan travel I was asked by the British Macedonian Relief Committee to act as their agent in the Ohrida Presba District. The Turkish Government gave permission and facilities. Our headquarters were at Monastir (now called Bitolj and included in

Yugoslavia, but at that time there were no Serbs there.) Our assistants, kavasses and interpreters were mostly Albanians obtained from the British and Foreign Bible Society which had a depot at Monastir. From them I learned of the strong nationalist spirit then at work. Without our capable and honest Albanian staff the work would have been far more difficult. The Governor of Ohrida, too, Mehdi Bey Frasheri, was an Albanian, a just and kindly man who was a great help to me. I regret to say he is now interned in Italy for having opposed the Italian invasion: may he live to see his land restored to independence. When the relief work was ended in the spring of 1904 my Albanian friends begged me not to return to England but to travel through Albania and see conditions for myself.

At this time the Turkish Government, afraid of the rising national spirit of the Albanians, tried to suppress it by forbidding the printing and teaching of the Albanian language under heavy penalties. Faik Bey of Konitza published an Albanian paper in London which was smuggled into the country. George Kyria, an employee of the Bible Society, prepared some books of the Bible in Albanian and the Society published them. The Society had leave to sell its publications in the Turkish Empire but the Turks had not reckoned on Albanian books. An Albanian colporteur was to try to sell these through the length of Albania. Would I go with him? I joined him at his home at Liaskovik. It was an inspiring journey. I first visited Koritza, Korcha as the Albanians call it. It was the active centre of the independence movement in South Albania, whose first object was to rid the land of all foreign influence.

A sister of George Kyrias, a brave and very capable woman, went to America aided by the American missionaries, was trained there and on her return was made mistress of a girls' school under the protection of the American Mission. She used American textbooks, gave her lessons in Albanian and destroyed all writing after the lesson.

The Turks searched vainly for the forbidden language. Christian and Moslem girls flocked to the school, learned to read and write and taught their brothers. All worked hard to counteract the influence of the Greek school and priests which the Turks permitted by way of suppressing Albanian. We went on, wherever we found an Albanian Governor we were welcome to sell as many books as we could. At Berati where there was a Turkish one all our Albanian books were confiscated but as we had a secret store awaiting us ahead this did not matter.

At Berati I first heard of the efforts being made by the priest, Fan Noli, to form an autocephalous Albanian Orthodox Church and free the land of Greek priests. At Berati the Christians complained that the Greek priest informed against persons possessing Albanian books. Fan Noli's long years of work were crowned with success after Albania became

Edith Durham

independent. The autocephalous Orthodox Albanian Church was legally established and there are now no Greek priests in Albania unless some have accompanied the invading Greek army. The clergy are all Albanian and their services are held in Albanian. The Head of the Church is Archbishop Kissi whose seat is at Tirana. The Church is thus on a par with those of the Serbs, Greeks and Bulgars, which are all autocephalous. Bishop Fan Noli is head of the Albanian colony in America.

I would emphasize the formation of the Albanian Orthodox Church as some newspapers describe the south Albanians as 'Greek Church' and its adherents as 'Greeks.' This is as incorrect as it would be to reckon all Roman Catholics as 'Italians.' Not only Christians but Moslems hastened to buy our books. At Elbasan in about an hour we sold seventy to Moslems. "Now," said a young gendarme joyfully, "I can teach my young brother to read." At Elbasan I found a movement to form a Uniate Church in order to stop Greek influence.

Thus we peddled books through all the towns of Albania and reached Scutari travel-worn but satisfied. There were then no made roads, the journey was on horseback, fording rivers where the horses nearly swam, plunging through marshy land where they were bogged to the shoulder and had to be dug out, and having to walk when the track was too bad to be safely ridden. Scutari was the centre of the independence movement in the north. Here there were more opportunities for education. Austria and Italy both coveted Albania and each tried to outdo the other in trying to win over the Albanians. So there were schools both for girls and boys, a boarding school for the mountain boys, a technical school and a printing press all under Austrian or Italian protection. The Albanians profited and studied eagerly.

Then came the Young Turk revolution in the summer of 1908. It promised freedom and equality for all. The Albanians played a major part in its first successes. The Kosovo men marched on Uskub (now called Skoplje but then a largely Albanian town). They evicted the old Turk governors from the district and occupied the town. Our Vice-Consul, a friend of the Albanians, testified to the good behaviour of the Albanian troops.

The Constitution was proclaimed, Scutari was wild with joy. Thousands of mountain men in finest array marched into the town, were feted and feasted. We fired revolvers (I had one in each hand) into the air till not a cartridge was left. Not an accident nor any disorder occurred. Said the French Vice-Consul: "What a people this would be with a good government!" They went back to their mountains happy and hopeful.

There was to be freedom of the press. Albanian newspapers sprang up like mushrooms in the night. Schools were opened with great rapidity. A Congress for the standardization of the alphabet and orthography was held at Monastir and a universal one adopted. The foreign schools had used separate systems. Long live Albania! She was to have her chance at last. Never again shall I see such joyous resurrection of a people.

I went over the mountains to Djakova which had long been closed to foreigners and over the Kosova plain to Prizren, Prishtina and Mitrovitza, back through Mirdita to Scutari. Everywhere the Albanians meant to have freedom.

Alas! The Young Turks made every possible blunder. Rightly handled the Albanians would have supported them as before against foes. But before the year was out the Albanians realized that no freedom was to be expected. I talked in vain to the two Young Turk Governors. Greece, Serbia, Bulgaria and Montenegro were all determined not to let the Young Turks succeed, for this would mean no more chance of land-grabbing. They formed the Balkan League to overthrow the Young Turk Government before it should have time to consolidate.

In 1910 the Albanians of Kosova revolted, being encouraged to do so by the Serbs who promised them help. They were led by the gallant Isa Boletin. Glad news came to Scutari. Isa had made terms with the Serbs. A Serb officer and his men were aiding him – even sharing quarters with him. Serbia had recognised Albania's right to independence. The age-long feud between Serb and Albanian was to cease. Isa believed and trusted the Serb and was cruelly deceived. The Serb in question was Colonel Dimitrijevitch, a leader of the gang which so brutally murdered King Alexander and Queen Draga in 1903, and head of the notorious Black Hand Society which planned a few years later the murder of the Archduke Franz Ferdinand and launched the First World War in 1914. One of the greatest criminals of his time. Disguised as Albanians, Dimitrijevitch and his men committed many murders, among them that of Popovitch, the Governor of Berani, who though a Montenegrin by birth was a supporter of the Young Turks and wished to make Berani a little model province. He was hacked to pieces and the crime was ascribed to the Albanians. But his widow, a Frenchwoman, declared to me that the Serbs had killed him. This revolt of the Albanians succeeded in completely alienating them from the Turks, as the Serbs intended it should do.

In 1911 the King of Montenegro offered to help the tribesmen of the Northern mountains to obtain freedom. They too believed him and rose. I was at Constantinople and returned in haste. The revolt was in full swing. King Nikola asked me to aid the crowd of women and children who had fled into Montenegro in wretched plight. Montenegro was supplying the rebels with arms, ammunition and advice. They put up a gallant fight but were crushed by the arrival of a large Turkish army. The Turkish Government ordered King Nikola to make peace at once. The dismay of the tribesmen whom he had promised to stand by till they were free was piteous. They were commanded to return at once to their burnt villages but refused. The situation was very critical and the Montenegrin government asked me to act as intermediary. They made it a condition that I should go with them. Mr. Charles Crane gave me £200, I raised more money and spent an arduous winter in relief work.

Then came the Balkan wars of 1912-13. By their cunning policy the Serbs had cruelly tricked the Albanians. They had separated them from the Turks and used them to drive the Turks from Kosovo. Far from fulfilling their promises to help the Albanians to liberty, the Serbs and Montenegrin armies fell upon them with ferocity. The Albanians were trapped and unable to obtain ammunition from either side. The Serbs ruthlessly massacred wholesale. In Montenegro, at the inn dinner table I heard a Serb officer boast how his men had slaughtered men, women and children of the Ljuma tribe. "You must kill the women," he said, "they breed men," and laughed till he choked over his beer. The Montenegrins cut off the lips and noses of prisoners and the dead and showed them as trophies, and burnt and looted. They boasted that when they took Scutari they would cut the throats of its inhabitants. The sad news came that Janina had fallen. Ismael Kemal, the Albanian leader in the south, appealed to the Powers and proclaimed the Independence of Albania, on November 28th 1912 at Valona. The claim of Albania was recognised and the Montenegrins were ordered to withdraw from the siege of Scutari. They obtained its surrender by means of a Quisling. Essad Pasha Toptani, a man detested save by the men of his own clan, was an officer in the Turkish army within Scutari. Terms were offered him through the medium of the Italian Consulate in Scutari. He and his men would be allowed to march out fully armed and he should be made Prince of a small Principality if he could contrive the surrender of the town. Essad then murdered the Turkish commander, Hussein Riza Bey, and admitted the Montenegrins just as the mountain men, who perceived too late how they had been tricked, were about to march to the town's relief. The Montenegrins set fire to the bazar and looted it. The Powers ordered the Montenegrins to clear out. They made a last and strange attempt to hold it. Petar Plamenatz, who had been made Governor, offered me the Governorship of Scutari – he to be nominal and I actual Governor – if I would persuade the tribesmen to ask for Montenegrin rule. "They will follow you," he said, "Speak the word, I implore." He offered bribes. "Impossible," said I. "But why?" "Because," I said sternly, "You have lied to me too often." He showed no anger. He said, "Alas, alas, Mlle. This time I swear I am telling the truth!"

An international naval force steamed up the river and as Admiral Burney landed the Montenegrin army marched out over the bridge.

Albania was saved. I spent the winter feeding and clothing the half-starved Scutarens and mountain folk.

The mountains were full of Moslem survivors escaped from the lands taken by the Montenegrins and Serbs, telling tales of horror. Men were roasted by fires to make them accept baptism. Women herded into church and their veils torn from them. If the poor, dazed victims did not answer next day to their Christian names they were beaten and in some cases raped. Two wretched widows told how the Serbs had cut the arteries of elbows and wrists and danced round while their victims bled to death. The grisly pantomime by which they described it made its truth clear. Briefly, the Serbs called this cleaning the land.

I did my best, too, to keep the peace among the foreign armies of occupation which arrived and had jurisdiction for some twelve miles round Scutari. Intrigue was rampant. Luckily in some crucial moments the tribesmen consulted me and I was able to get them to listen to the Admiral which enraged some foreign officers.

Mr. Nevinson, the well-known war correspondent and Mr. Eriksen, an American missionary, arrived and asked me to ride with them through Albania. We found perfect order kept by small provisional government in every town and were welcomed everywhere. There was dread of Essad the traitor and hopes that soon the Powers would send the promised King.

We went to Ohrida, where large Serb forces were making ready to fight the Bulgars, and thence to Koritza, where we went to the schoolhouse. Heavy Greek forces occupied the town. Orders were being given that shop fronts were to be painted Greek colours. We were hailed as saviours. The Greeks held the telegraph lines and Koritza was cut off from the world. Save us from the Greeks we were implored. We visited the Greek commander, Colonel Kondoulis. He made no concealment of his intention not only to keep Koritza but to take the whole of South Albania up to Tepeleni, as he showed on a map. I protested that the lands were wholly Albanian and he had no right whatever to them. He replied, "Appetite comes with eating. We have eaten and shall eat more!" I said, "He that eats too much gets the belly-ache." Nevinson said "Take care, those fellows are furious."

On returning to the schoolhouse – the Greeks had closed the school – we learned that Greek soldiers were making a house to house visit, ordering every inhabitant to come to a public meeting to vote for what form of government they wished. This was obviously arranged to impress us. Lest we should be made tools of and put on the platform with the Greeks, we went out and the officer sent to fetch us was too late. We arrived late at the meeting. Surrounded by Greek troops the populace was said to have voted unanimously to be Greek and a telegram to that effect was sent to the ambassadors' conference in London. From both without and within the town we were begged to save them. We hired a guide and started on a two and a half days' ride over rough mountain tracks to Berati, which was in Albanian hands. Nevinson drafted a telegram explaining how the Greek vote had been obtained, Koritza was allotted to Albania and saved. At Valona we were met with a deputation of fine fellows from the Chiameria, also occupied by the Greeks, who begged earnestly to be saved but their prayer was in vain.

I left Albania for Christmas, 1913, and returned to Durazzo in April 1944, where the Powers of Europe had appointed the Prince zu Wied as King. Why they agreed to choose him is a mystery, since France, Russia, Italy, the Greeks and the Serbs had agreed together to expel him and permit no German influence in Albania. Wied was a well-meaning man but was never given a chance. He fell into the hands of the traitor Essad Pasha, who went to meet him and so gained his confidence that he made Essad his Minister of War. I landed at Durazzo to find a whirlpool of intrigue. The French Commissioner, a Polish Jew born in Bosnia (Krajewsky), told me that France would never permit an Independent Albania; a Russian journalist and Dr. Dillon were backing Essad. I had a long talk with Wied and begged him not to trust Essad but to make a tour of the country with me. He hesitated too long. Essad as War Minister had control of the arms; he armed the men of his own district and also a large force of refugees from Dibra, which had been given to the Serbs. They were told that if they would expel Wied, Dibra would be returned to them. They rose, the signal for the attack being by an Italian, Colonel Muriccio, waving a red lantern at night. The British Vice-Consul saw him and he was arrested. So was Essad, who ought to have been court-martialled and shot. The Italians made a great uproar, Muricchio had to be released and Wied feared to act. Each of the Powers had a warship lying of Durazzo and Essad was put on board the Austrian warship. The Italians claimed him and cleared decks for action. The world war might have begun then had not Austria released Essad, who was taken by the Italians to Rome, feted and decorated.

The attack on Durazzo was a failure in spite of Italian efforts. The town was well defended by the little body of Dutch gendarmerie appointed by the Powers as Wied's guard. The rebels sued for truce but hardly was truce made when there came news that the Greeks were invading south Albania and that Koritza was threatened. Sir Harry Lamb, The British Commissioner, sent me to Valona to investigate. It was too true. The Greeks and Serbs had planned a simultaneous attack. The refugees were streaming down to the coast. Valona was thronged. Under every tree or shelter for miles around men, women and children were falling exhausted from a flight for life from their burning villages. The detachment of

Dutch gendarmes who were in charge of Koritza had resisted till overwhelmed by superior forces and then had fled with the rest. They gave terrible accounts of the sufferings and deaths that occurred in the rush over the mountains.

Athens, when remonstrated with, denied complicity and declared it to be a local rising of so called 'Christian Epirots' against the Moslems. This was quite untrue; the local Christians did all they could to aid their Moslem brethren. As Sir Harry Lamb said, the so-called Epirots were in fact Cretans. The leader was a Greek, Zographos.

An International Committee of which I was a member, toiled to save the starving, suffering people. I shall never forget the miserable children dying under the trees. I obtained but very little condensed milk and there were at very least fifty thousand refugees. A small ration of bread per head per day was the most we could do.

The Greeks were said to be approaching Valona. Where the army was we did not know. Athens continued to deny its existence. So I went myself two days' ride up country to spy its position. Not far from Tepeleni on the opposite side of a deep valley when I crawled along the mountainside, I saw through field-glasses, a large military camp with soldiers in khaki, tents and horses, as unlike a band of local revolutionaries as could well be imagined.

I returned in hot haste in one day, hoping to put pressure on Athens, and found that Russia and Germany had declared war. The Great War had begun. Austria's declaration of war on Serbia was greeted with wild joy by the Albanians. The Serbs would be justly punished for the murder of the Archduke and Kosova would be restored to Albania. We were cut off from all news. I crossed to Brindisi to get news, meaning to return if all was well and learned to my dismay that we had declared war forty-eight hours earlier. There was nothing for it but to return to England.

The Serb attack on Albania ceased . . . the Italians landed at Valona and stopped the Greek advance . . . the French occupied Koritza, proclaiming a Republic. During the war, though Albania had been declared neutral and independent by the Powers, it was entered by Serb, Montenegrin, French, Austrian, Italian and British troops. The Prince of Wied left on September 3rd and Essad returned. By now the rebels saw how they had been tricked and telegraphed to Wied to return; he never did.

In April 1915, the British Government made a secret treaty by which Albania was to be divided between Greece and the Serbs, Essad to have his Principality. He acted as French Agent all through and was well paid. The secret treaty was published by the Bolsheviks in 1917. Colonel the Hon. Aubrey Herbert formed a strong committee to struggle for Albania's independence: Sir Samuel Hoare, Lord Moyne and Lord Harlech were members of it; I was honorary secretary. We had the support of Lord Cecil and later of Lord Balfour. After much hard work Albania was again made an independent state and a member of the League of Nations but unfortunately the Serbs were permitted to retain territory with some eight hundred thousand Albanians, and the Greeks also retained the wholly Albanian Chiameria.

Both Serb and Greek reckoned the Moslems as Turks, expropriated them and expelled them in numbers, penniless, to Turkey. Not a single Albanian school has been provided for those that remain. Their numbers have been so reduced as to make them powerless and they have been deprived of civil rights in Greece.

When I returned to Albania in 1921, a council of three Regents was ruling at the head of a Parliament. all seemed going smoothly; there was no national debt; Essad dared not claim his principality and to make sure that he should not do so, a young Albanian shot him in Paris, where he was living on French money. The outlook was hopeful and there was perfect order.

But oil was the undoing of Albania. It was believed to exist in large quantities. The wise priest Fan Noli thought it better for Albania to remain poor for a time than to grant large oil concessions to foreign powers. Others favoured getting rich quickly. Ahmet Zogu of Mati, now known as King Zog and Fan Noli's rival for the Presidency, promised a big concession to the Anglo-Persian Oil Company and one to Italy. He obtained the support of Great Britain and the Anglo-Persian started boring.

In memory of her son, Aubrey Herbert, Elizabeth Lady Carnarvon started her noble work. She equipped a hospital at Valona, built and equipped a library, sent a scoutmaster to start boy scouts, which were very popular, and began anti-malarial work. British officers were appointed to train the gendarmerie. All looked well. Alas the Anglo-Persian found no oil worth working and withdrew. Italy, on the contrary, found good oil. Had we obtained the concession which the Italians did, Albania's fate would have been very different. As it was, it became Italy's sphere of influence. The boy scouts were first suppressed and finally the British officers dismissed, Italy undertook to finance Albania and to make roads and bridges. Albania, which at first thought of Italy as a protection against Greeks and Serbs, became uneasy as Italy dug her claws in deeper and deeper. Some attempts to resist, made by the rising generation, many of whom had been educated abroad, were suppressed.

Then came the fatal Good Friday, when we all looked on and let a huge mechanized force overwhelm the little land and presented Italy with the control of the Straits of Otranto. At Durazzo the gendarmerie and the cadets bombarded the tiny town and forced a landing. A pathetic incident was that when planes flew over Tirana the populace thought they were English planes coming to their rescue. But they dropped leaflets saying that if further resistance were offered the town would be destroyed. Having no anti-aircraft guns – none could be offered.

Very briefly this is the sad tale of a small and fine people who want to live their own lives on their own land. Should any further dismemberment of their lands take place they are threatened with extinction, for neither neighbour has shown them any mercy.

In the years when I lived among them I found the Albanians loyal, grateful and kindly. That they are highly intelligent is proved by the fact that those who have managed to come to England for education have taken good degrees at the London University. Their beautiful silver work and fine embroideries show them to be offered up as a human sacrifice, either to appease our foes or propitiate our allies.

M.E.D.

Edith Durham, 'Queen of the Mountains.' Kralica e Malësorëvet.

33
THE CORFU INCIDENT

Article by Tim Butcher, Defence Correspondent.
The Daily Telegraph. 28th October 1996

Britain returns Albania's gold in £1.3m deal

A diplomatic impasse dating from the start of the Cold War will end today when one and a half tons of gold worth around £12m and held for fifty years in the Bank of England is returned to the government of Albania.

Britain had blocked the gold's return until Albania accepted responsibility for the death of forty-four Royal Navy sailors killed in 1946 when two destroyers hit mines in the straits between Corfu and Albania.

After lengthy diplomatic negotiations since Albania's communist dictatorship ended in 1991, an agreement was reached to return the gold for payment to Britain of compensation.

The bullion, stolen from the Albanian central bank by the Axis powers during the 1939-45 war, has been held in the Bank of England since 1945.

At a private ceremony scheduled to be held at the Foreign Office in Whitehall today representatives of the Albanian Central Bank will receive a document giving them a title to the gold.

The Albanians will hand over to the British Government a warrant for £1.3m compensation.

Veterans of the 'Corfu incident' criticised the exchange as the compensation was one tenth of the £13m awarded to Britain by the International Court of Justice in 1951.

"The sum sounds pretty paltry when you think of the loss of two ships, of forty-four lives and fifty years of pursuing the claim," said Sir Donald Gosling, the joint chairman of National Car Parks who was a seventeen-year-old signaller on a cruiser accompanying the two damaged destroyers.

"But I suppose fifty years is a long time and honour has been done if only to allow Albania to continue its slow reform towards being a democratic country."

A spokesman for the Foreign Office said the principle of liability had been accepted by Albania, which has a weak economy that is developing slowly.

"The government has great sympathy with the families of those who suffered in the incident but they did receive compensation from the British government shortly after the incident."

The issue of the Albanian bullion, known as King Zog's gold after the last Albanian monarch, has soured relations between Britain and Albania since the incident involving the two ships, Saumarez and Volage.

Albania dismissed British claims that the mines were illegal and there was some evidence that they might have been laid by Yugoslav naval forces.

But a hearing at the International Court of Justice in the Hague supported Britain's claim and awarded compensation.

When Albania refused to pay, Britain blocked Albania's claim for the return of gold looted under Nazi occupation.

The gold was part of a large cache of Nazi gold held in the Bank of England but administered by a joint commission consisting of Britain, France and America.

While the commission returned vast sums of gold to nine claimant countries such as Austria and Luxembourg, Britain blocked the Albanian claim until the issue of damages for the Corfu incident was settled.

Present at the historic ceremony at the Foreign Office in Whitehall was His Excellency Pavli Qesku, Albanian Ambassador to Great Britain.

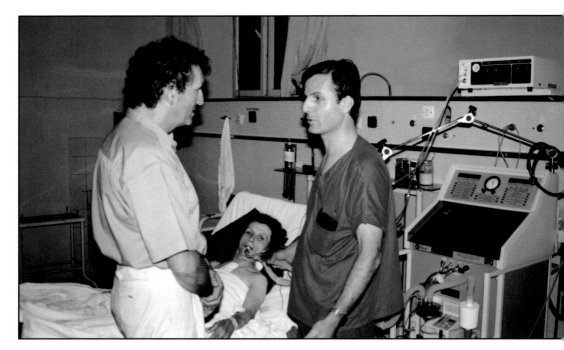

Dr. Roland Xhaxho on 18th June 1992 receiving Albania's first jet ventilator. It arrived just in time to save the life of Fatime Hasani, who was suffering from a collapsed lung condition.

A humble moment indeed, just after the presentation of The Order of Mother Teresa to Bhasker Solanki, John Arthur, John van Weenen and Bill Hamilton in Tirana.

34
EPILOGUE

With the termination of all 'TFA's humanitarian aid trips to Albania, stretching over a period of six years in which thirty-one missions were undertaken involving the safe delivery of an estimated seven million pounds-worth of aid, one has to ask the inevitable question – Was it worth it?

Of course the answer is an unequivocal 'Yes' – but pause for just a moment to consider the downside.

The second question that needs to be answered is – why on earth should any human being risk his or her life trying to save someone they don't know and would never otherwise come into contact with?

On the surface, it defies all reasoning and logic yet paradoxically, makes a powerful appeal to two very basic human instincts, those of compassion and benevolence.

The third question and probably the most pointed that charity workers are sometimes asked is – why are you doing it? Occasionally, such questions have been known to clearly carry unpleasant undertones implying – 'what's in it for you?' I answer simply, I do it for me and secondly for them.

Fortunately, there are a vast number of wonderful people in Great Britain and to many of these, 'TFA' will always be indebted.

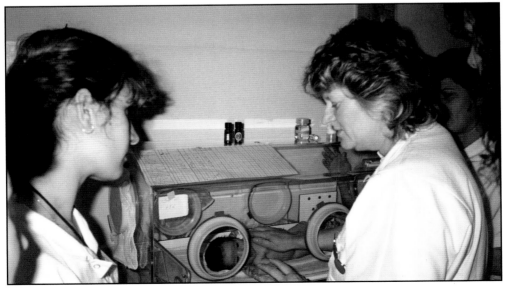

Carol Rowley demonstrating 'bonding techniques' for mothers and babies to doctors at Tirana's maternity hospital.

Looking back, it is interesting to see how timing and fate played a hand in the scheme of things.

The malnourished form of Jessica Nexhipi was shown to me at exactly the right time and 21st September 1991 remains indelibly imprinted on my mind. Had I not switched on the television set at precisely 7.30 a.m., 'TFA' might possibly never have come into being.

The seven hundred and forty tonne convoy, the largest to leave Britain since World War Two would, in all probability, never have materialised and many people in central and northern Albania could quite possibly have perished.

A further irony was this.

After meeting Sali Berisha for the first time by chance, (or was it fate?) in Blackpool and subsequently being invited to Albania 'to see for myself' the appalling conditions, the link between 'TFA' and the Democratic Party strengthened. Consequently, it was through this that a distribution network was set in motion. It worked well and the people benefited, and a year later when it came to voting in the General Election, the people remembered or were conveniently reminded, which party had helped them in their hour of need.

Some months later Dr. Sali Berisha was installed in office as President of the Republic and one evening he observed that 'TFA,' in no small measure, had inadvertently been responsible for changing the course of history – it was a sobering thought and a great compliment.

Throughout the 1991-1997 period, we met people from all levels of society, from the poorest of the poor who had very little but insisted on sharing what they had with us, to the intelligentsia and those in high office who were equally as generous.

'TFA's aid deployment was both wide and varied but the main thrust of our efforts was directed towards the poorest folk, in the north and north east of the country. It was there, in Malsia e Madhe (The Great Highlands) we discovered villages and communes as inaccessible as they were deprived, where most inhabitants had never seen a foreigner before.

In Kruma, near Kukes in the north east, Alan Bristow discovered abject poverty and despite his vast humanitarian experience – returned a changed man. Carol Rowley, normally found in her Heald Green surgery in Manchester giving remedial massage for clients with sports injuries, suddenly found herself alone in the remote eastern Albanian village of Qeshit teaching bonding techniques for mothers with young babies.

Carolyn O'Donnell, a schoolteacher from Parkfields School in Toddington, Bedfordshire was delighted to hand out warm winter clothing to the freezing children of Peshkopia and Bushat, all collected and paid for by her school pupils. Irene Leslie, Azad Kumar, Alan Blake and Darren Gill were deeply saddened by conditions they found in the village of Barbe near Librazd. The villagers fortitude and generosity inspired Irene especially, who now spends a big part of her life working voluntarily for 'TFA' in the capacity of honorary secretary.

Every team needs an anchorman – someone who is always there and can be depended upon. 'TFA' has been fortunate indeed to have just such a man – Alan Blake, who, when not delivering humanitarian aid can be located near Oxford in his nine to five job at the Royal Mail.

Ordinary people in ordinary jobs? Well – jobs perhaps, but presided over by some very extraordinary people.

A not so ordinary man who accompanied me to Albania in 1993 was Bob Poynton the renowned karate teacher from Liverpool. At Tirana hospital Bob's attention was drawn to a twelve year old girl who was suffering from a heart condition. She was doomed to an inactive life, as no treatment was available to her in Albania. Her parents had just 'left her' in hospital and disappeared back to Saranda, with no intention of returning.

As Bob sat by her bed, holding her hand, an idea was formulating in his mind. He knew the chief cardiologist at Liverpool Royal Infirmary.

Four weeks later, she arrived in Liverpool accompanied by Dr. Lindita Agolli. The operation was a success. Although the surgeon made no charge whatsoever, a sum of three thousand pounds had to be raised to cover all expenses for the trip.

Bob Poynton paid every penny!

Bob Poynton with Sulejman Zhugli in September 1993.

Another person whom I have great respect for is Sali Berisha. As a great man once said, "By their deeds shall ye know them." Prior to 1991, Dr. Berisha was an eminent cardiologist and the World Health Organisation representative for Albania. In going against the communist authority in the defence of his medical students, he undoubtedly risked his life on more than one occasion. After the massacre at Shkodra of three students and a senior Democratic Party official, his country called upon him to lead them. There was no other man who could do it and the pressures on him were enormous.

During the five years that followed, and it should never be forgotten, he achieved a tremendous amount for Albania. As the Patron of 'TFA' he never once refused us help or assistance and I have to say I am very proud to be able to call him a friend, as too his wife Liri, son Shkelzen and daughter Argita.

Despite the many accusations levelled at him during the latter part of his Presidency, I still believe he is, and remains an honest man. Perhaps his biggest mistake was not ridding himself of the corrupt or disloyal politicians that may have surrounded him.

In writing this book, I have attempted to tell the true story of **Task Force Albania** from its inception to the conclusion of its humanitarian relief work. My words have been augmented by those of others to give the reader a more rounded picture of Europe's poorest country, and events that have taken place there.

For me, the charity's undoubted achievements have been overshadowed by the people who made them possible. Had it not been for The Great British public responding so magnificently to appeals for aid, 'TFA' may have fallen at the first hurdle. Accordingly – when the individual continuously sees on television appalling pictures of violence and deprivation, he or she feels unable to respond in any meaningful way saying, "What can I do? Why doesn't the Government do something." As often as not, they feel quite helpless.

The truth is of course, the individual *can* make a difference and this book is all about a small group of people who did just that. Ordinary people in ordinary jobs who made the effort, got off their backsides and did something.

Finally – let me turn to the future.

With the need for humanitarian aid receding and a newly elected Socialist Government, in favour of a free market economy, in power, the time has come for 'TFA' to move on. The obvious avenue is one of development and the charity, in conjunction with its sister foundation in Albania, 'Child Smile,' is embarking on a most ambitious programme that will create in years to come a National Albanian Library Network for children.

Most would agree the country's future lies in the hands of its children. Their education is vital in creating new thinking, knowledge and self respect. *At present, there are very few lending libraries in Albania*, making it almost impossible for a child to borrow a book.

'TFA's feasibility study indicated an overwhelming need and recommended a three phase approach:

Phase 1

The creation of the First National Children's Library in Tirana for its two hundred and fifty thousand children.

It is intended to dedicate the National Children's Library to the late Diana, Princess of Wales.

Phase 2

The creation of children's libraries in provincial cities based on the national model in Tirana.

Carolyn O'Donnell spent much of her time at the maternity hospital dressing the babies in their first clothes. For just one moment I thought I detected that 'broody' look! Terry, take note!!!

Phase 3

The setting up of a mobile library network to service rural and mountainous regions.

A massive fundraising scheme is under way in Great Britain whereby

The 'TFA' team: left to right, Alan Blake, Carol Rowley, Carolyn O'Donnell, Alan Bristow and the author.

twenty-five thousand schools have been contacted asking each child to give 'a book and a pound.' The idea is as ingenious as it is simple and with English being the number one foreign language in Albania, the pounds will help to build the National Library, whilst the books will stock its shelves.

Rotary International, Inner Wheel Clubs and The Salvation Army have all thrown their weight behind the schemes nationally and meetings have taken place in Tirana with the Albanian Government and the EU office discussing financial support and subsidies.

Sphresa Vreto, the leading Albanian authoress, has agreed to become the Library's Principal and she will be backed up by economist Tatjana Zhugli and concert pianist Luiza Dhamo. Adjoining the main building will be a bookshop for retail sales and a large seated area that will serve as a concert room/seminar and conference centre. This facility will be available for public hire and together with the bookshop, will enable the National Library to be self-financing.

In conclusion, may I say writing this book has truly been a labour of love. I have enjoyed every minute of it.

However, by now the reader will be only too aware of my limited knowledge of the English language and my inability to express myself as comprehensively and articulately as I would wish. Nevertheless, I have genuinely attempted to mutilate the English language 'as little as possible,' but no doubt, the book will be littered from cover to cover with numerous grammatical errors etc., for which I hereby apologise most profusely.

Leaving secondary school at fourteen years of age and being told by the headmaster "You'll never amount to anything" may not have helped but it certainly reinforced the message. Sadly, his words stayed with me for close on fifty years.

Using a 'ghost writer' was never an option I entertained. It had to be 'warts an' all.'

Any help I was able to give the Albanian people over the past seven years is negligible compared to what I have received back and I feel very privileged to have been given a chance to make that small contribution.

Looking ahead to our new project, I am filled with that almost forgotten boyhood emotion – anticipation. It's like lying in bed waiting for Santa Claus to come and listening for his sleigh bells. Confucius was right when he said "A journey of a thousand miles begins with the first step."

For 'TFA' that first step has already been taken and with each passing day, we move inexorably closer to our dream – and our mission statement becoming a reality:

To give the poorest children of Albania *hope* and a *chance* to realise their full potential.

As has previously been mentioned in chapter seventeen, it was on a September day, on a train to Darjeeling, that Albania's most famous daughter received her 'inner command.' The message was quite clear Mother Teresa explained, pointing her finger, there was no doubt whatsoever – "it was an order."

"God wanted me to be poor and to love him in the distressing guise of the poorest of the poor."

For more than fifty years she did just that; a truly remarkable woman and an inspiration to us all.

As I left her, she slipped a small card into my hand which she had signed. It was simple, unpretentious yet its message was profound.

I felt very humble indeed.

The fruit of SILENCE is Prayer
The fruit of PRAYER is Faith
The fruit of FAITH is Love
The fruit of LOVE is Service
The fruit of SERVICE is Peace

God bless you Mother Teresa

After reading this book, should you wish to make a donation to the fund for building the National Children's Library you are most welcome to contact the author by writing to:

The Priory, Wollaston, Northamptonshire NN29 7SL, England.
Kindly make cheques payable to 'Task Force Albania' only.
'TFA' is a registered charity in Great Britain, reg no. 1015236

Thank you, most sincerely.

Dedication of The National Children's Library to the late Diana, Princess of Wales

In November 1996, Diana, Princess of Wales watched a video at Kensington Palace of 'TFA's work in Albania. Moved by scenes depicting the plight of orphaned children, she expressed a strong interest in visiting the country on a future mission.

In dedicating the National Library to her memory, we at 'TFA' pay respect to a great humanitarian.

THE TEAM

Shpresa Vreto
*The Library's Principal.
Authoress and Literary
figure.*

Luiza Dhamo
Concert Pianist

Tatjana Zhugli
Economist

Architect: **Mr. Krist Andon**

Lawyer: **Mr. Fatmir Lacej**

Missio

*"To give the poorest childre
to realise*

incess of Wales

LIBRARY OF ALBANIA

THE LOCATION

3rd Floor
The International Culture Centre
Bulevardi 'Deshmoret e Kombit'
Tirana
Albania

THE CHARITY

UNITED KINGDOM

'Task Force Albania'
Reg. Charity No. 1015236

THE FOUNDATION

ALBANIA

'Child Smile'
'Buzeqeshja Feminore'
Reg. Albanian NGO Forum

Executive Director:
John van Weenen

tement

ania hope and a chance
potential"

35
THE ALBANIAN PEOPLE'S ASSEMBLY

The following information has been included for the benefit of British charities and Non Governmental Organisations (NGOs) working in Albania. It was issued on 25th July 1997, twenty-six days after the election of 29th June 1997.

The new cabinet was approved by the President of the republic, Prof. Dr. Rexhep Mejdani.

The Albanian People's Assembly elected Skender Gjinushi as their speaker and Namik Dokie as his deputy.

Composition of the Cabinet.

Prime Minister	Fatos Nano	SP
Deputy Prime Minister	Bashkim Fino	SP
Foreign Affairs	Paskal Milo	SDP
Defence	Sabit Brokaj	SP
Home	Neritan Ceka	DAP
Public Economy & Privatisation	Ylli Bufi	SP
Labour, Social Affairs & Women	Elmaz Sherifi	SP
Agriculture & Food	Lufter Xhuveli	AP
Finance	Arben Malaj	SP
Trade & Tourism	Shaqir Vukaj	SP
Public Works & Transport	Gaqo Apostoli	SDP
Education & Science	Et'hem Ruka	SP
Culture, Youth & Sports	Arta Dade	SP
Health & Environment	Leonard Solis	HRUP
Minister of State for Legislative Reform & Relations with People's Assembly	Arben Imami	DAP
Minister of State for Economic Co-operation & Development	Ermelinda Meksi	SP
Justice	Thimio Kondi	Independent
Secretary of State for Euro-Atlantic Integration	Maqo Lakrori	SP
Secretary of State for Defence Policy	Perikli Teta	DAP
Home Secretary of State	Ndre Legisi	SP
Secretary of State for Local Government	Lush Perpali	SP

*	SP	Socialist Party
*	SDP	Social-Democratic Party
*	DAP	Democratic Alliance Party
*	HRUP	Human Rights Union Party
*	AP	Agrarian Party
*	DP	Democratic Party

Changes within the Cabinet as at 15th June 1998:

Deputy Prime Minister and Minister of Government Coordination	Kastriot Islami	SP
Deputy Prime Minister and Minister of Local Government	Bashkim Fino	SP
Minister of Public Order	Perikli Teta	DAP
Minister of Defence	Luan Hajdaraga	SP
Minister of Labour and Social Affairs	Anastas Angjeli	SP
Minister of Culture, Youth and Sports	Edi Rama	Independent
Secretary of State of European Integration at the Ministry of Foreign Affairs	Ilir Meta	SP

36
BRITISH CHARITIES, NGOs AND INDIVIDUALS ASSISTING ALBANIA

I n the last seven years and especially since Bill Hamilton's graphic news bulletins in September 1991, an amazing thing has happened. Scores, if not hundreds of ordinary people, after watching his BBC reports were moved into taking action themselves.

Most of them, myself included, quite simply had no idea where Albania was. Yet countless Britons downed tools, acquired a transit van or similar vehicle, loaded it with food and black bin liners full of clothes and headed for Dover.

Bill's report and Bhasker Solanki's pictures were compelling viewing and I'm certain, provided much of the motivation necessary.

Many of the groups listed here are still working in Albania today. Those included are the ones I know of and I apologise to all those omitted through ignorance on my part:

CHILDRENS AID DIRECT, (incorporating Education Aid). David Grubb, 1 Priory Avenue, Caversham, Reading, Berkshire, RG4 7SE. 01734 464444.

ADRA Trans Europe. John Arthur, 119 St. Peter's Street, St. Albans, Herts. Al1 3EY. 01727 860331.

TASK FORCE ALBANIA. John van Weenen, The Priory, Wollaston, Northants NN29 7SL. 01933 663725.

BRITISH RED CROSS. Chris Holdsworth, 9 Grosvenor Crescent, London SW1X 7EJ. 0171 2355454.

ALBANIAN CHILDREN'S AID. Revd Dr. John Walmsley, Unit 2, Thirsk Industrial Park, Thirsk, North Yorkshire YO7 3BX. 01845 526272.

SAVE THE CHILDREN. Matthew Bullard, 17 Grove Lane, London SE5 8RD. 0171 703 5400.

OXFAM. Douglas Saltmarshe, 274 Banbury Road, Oxford. OX2 7DZ, 01865 312297.

EAST EUROPEAN PARTNERSHIP. Tanya Barron, 15 Princeton

Court, 53-55 Filsham Road, London SW15 1AZ. 0181 780 2841.

VOLUNTARY SERVICES OVERSEAS. David Green, 317 Putney Bridge Road, London, SW15 2PN. 0181 780 2266.

CHILDHOPE UK. Nikolas Fenton, 40 Rosebury Avenue, London EC1R 4RN. 0171 833 2266.

MENCAP. John Payne, 123 Golden Lane, London EC17 0RT. 0171 454 0454.

OCKENDON VENTURE. Ailsa Moore, Guildford Road, Woking, Surrey. GU22 7UU. 01483 772012.

LIGHTFORCE INTERNATIONAL. George R. Ridley, Christian Centre, Oldbrook, Milton Keynes MK6 2TG. 01908 670655.

GLOBAL CARE. Peter Burnett, PO Box 61, Coventry, CV5 6AX. 01203 602203.

THE TRAINING TRUST. Pauline McCabe, 145 Great Charles Street, Birmingham, B3 3JR. 0121 200 1140.

SCOTTISH ALBANIAN APPEAL. Annette Beuth, 23a Dalmeny Street, Leith, Edinburgh, EH6 8PQ. 0131 555 6411.

SHETLAND AID TO ALBANIA. Joanne Adamson, Virdaklee, Cunningsburgh, Shetland, ZE2 9HG. 01950 3334.

SKYE AID TO ALBANIA. Dr. Alan Humphrey, Corriegorm, Broadford, Isle of Skye, IV49 4AB. 01471 822515.

SUSSEX AID TO ALBANIA. Roy and Hilary Loosely, Blackboys Nursery, Blackboys, Nr Uckfield, East Sussex. TN22 5JX. 01825 890858.

WOOTTON BASSET ALBANIA APPEAL. Martyn Giles, The Woodshaw Inn, Woodshaw, Wootton Basset, Swindon, SN4 8RB. 01793 854617.

CHALLENGE ALBANIA. Sarah Ashman, New Barn Farm, Bucklebury, Reading, Berks. RG7 6EF. 01734 712579.

HALLELUJAH MINISTRIES. Kevin Bidwell, 'Havenvale', 100 School Road, Sheffield, S31 8QJ. 01909 770996.

ALBANIA AID APPEAL. Chris Blake, 200 Marlow Bottom, Marlow, Bucks. SL7 3PR. 01628 472220.

NORTH-WEST ALBANIAN APPEAL. Tom Brennan, 2 The Strand, Ashton-in-Makerfield, Gt. Manchester, WN4 8LD. 01942 720648.

AID FOR ALBANIA. Joe Medhurst, 59a Farmdale Road, Lancaster, LA1 4JB. 01524 60755.

ALBANIAN MEDICAL RELIEF APPEAL. Allan Stokes, 30 Liverpool Road South, Maghull, Liverpool, L31 7BW. 0151 520 1025.

ALBANIAN RELIEF PROJECT. Caroline Dover, Sunderland Christian Centre, Hendon Road, Sunderland, Tyne and Wear, SR1 2HX. 0191 514 5759.

BEDWORTH AID FOR ALBANIA. Gary Spicer, Bulkington Road, Bedworth, Warwickshire, CV12 9DC. 01203 317835.

BRITISH-ALBANIAN LAW ASSOCIATION. Babette Brown, The Law Society, 50 Cnancery Lane, London, WC2A 1SX. 0171 242 1222.

CANAAN CHRISTIAN CENTRE. Andy Gilmour, Canaan Christian Centre, Staines, Middlesex. TW18 4PD. 01784 441040.

IRISH AID TO ALBANIA. Mary Linders, The Quay, Portrane, Donabate, Co. Dublin. 010 353 1 8436359.

KOSOVA AID. Agron Loxha, 132 Buckingham Palace Road, London SW1W 9SA. 0171 730 1050.

SOS ALBANIA. Sister Anita MacDonald, 33 Mattock Lane, Ealing, London W5. 0181 567 1464.

MIDLANDS TO ALBANIA. Dragan Stajka, 399 Warwick Road, Solihull, Birmingham, B91 9BJ. 0121 705 2432.

ORCADIAN MOVEMENT. Lynn Barbour, 1 Silver Knowes Load, Edinburgh EH4 5HR. 0131 336 4268.

DORSET AID TO ALBANIA. Lars Wicks, Rosegarth, Valley Road, Harmans Cross, Swanage, Dorset, BH19 3DX. 01929 480878.

BRITISH AID FOR DEPRIVED CHILDREN. Brenda Belton, Oakdale, Little London Lane, West Cowick, Goole, North Humberside DN14 9EG. 01405 861024.

ALBANIAN VILLAGE RELIEF GROUP. Barry Wigglesworth, 353 Beccles Road, Carlton Colville, Lowestoft, Suffolk. 01502 572085.

999 TO ALBANIA. Nigel Donkin, 18 Rectory Road, Rowhedge, Colchester, Essex CO5 7HR. 01206 729477.

CHILDREN IN CRISIS. Deborah Oxley, 5d Calico House, Plantation Wharf, York Road, London SW11 3UB 0171 978 5001.

OTHER USEFUL ADDRESSES;
ANGLO-ALBANIAN ASSOCIATION
An association to foster friendships between the peoples of Britain and Albania.

Hon. Secretary and Treasurer: Denys Salt, Flat 6, 38 Holland Park, London, W11 3RP. 0171 727 0287.

ALBANIAN EMBASSY.
His Excellency Agim Fagu – Albanian Ambassador, 4th Floor, 38 Grosvenor Gdns., London SW1W 0EB. 0171 730 5709.
Fax. 0171 730 5747.

FRIENDS OF ALBANIA SOCIETY.
Hon. Secretary: Primrose Peacock, 'Peasacre', Thurloxton, Taunton, Somerset, TA2 8RJ. 01823 412452.

37
BIBLIOGRAPHY

RECOMMENDED READING

TRAVELLERS GUIDE TO ALBANIA
Agim Neza. Published by Aco. UK. Princes Risborough, Aylesbury, 1993.
BLUE GUIDE ALBANIA.
James Pettifer. Published by A & C Black, London, 1994.
ALBANIA WHO CARES.
Bill Hamilton, Bhasker Solanki. Published by Autumn House, Grantham, 1992. ISBN 1-873796-18-8.
SOME TRIBAL ORIGINS LAWS AND CUSTOMS OF THE BALKANS.
M E Durham. Published by George Allen and Unwin Ltd. London 1928.
ALBANIA AND THE ALBANIANS.
Derek Hall. Published by Pinter Publishers Ltd. London 1994.
THE ALBANIANS. Europe's Forgotten Survivors.
Anton Logoreci. First published 1977 by Victor Gollancz, then by Westview Press, Colorado, 1978.
HIGH ALBANIA.
M E Durham, Published by Edward Arnold, London 1909.
THE BURDEN OF THE BALKANS.
M E Durham. Published Edward Arnold, London, 1905.
THROUGH THE LAND OF THE SERBS.
M E Durham. Published by Edward Arnold, London 1904.
20 YEARS OF BALKAN TANGLE.
M E Durham. Published by George Allen and Unwin, London 1920.
THE STRUGGLE FOR SCUTARI.
M E Durham. Published by Edward Arnold, London 1914.

BY THE SAME AUTHOR
THE BEGINNERS GUIDE TO SHOTOKAN KARATE John van Weenen 7th Dan. First published 1983. ISBN 0 9517660 2 3.
ADVANCED SHOTOKAN KARATE KATA Vol. 1. John van Weenen 7th Dan. First published 1984 ISBN 0 9517660 1 5.

"The marvellous richness of human experience would lose something of rewarding joy if there were not limitations to overcome. The hilltop hour would not be half so wonderful if there were no dark valleys to traverse."

Helen Keller